The sentinel of early morning is the Morehead-Patterson Bell Tower, surely silent now, but capable of a great voice with its dozen bells of 300 to 3,500 pounds each.

Chip Henderson

Chip Henderson

Library of Congress Catalogue Number: 87-071526

Hardcover ISBN: 0-917631-04-8

Printed in Japan by Dai Nippon Printing Co., Ltd. Color separations by Dai Nippon Printing Co., Ltd.

Typography by TypEsthetics, Raleigh, N.C.

Published by Capitol Broadcasting Company, Inc., Raleigh, N.C.

Steve Muir

THE UNIVERSITY OF
NORTH
CAROLINA
AT CHAPEL HILL

The First 200 Years

Editor-in-Chief Hugh Morton, Jr.

Associate Editor Jane Collins

Photographic Editor Chip Henderson, Henderson/Muir Photography

Assistant Photographic Editor Steve Muir, Henderson/Muir Photography

Designer Russell Avery, Avery Designs

Chip Henderson

Carolina springs. . . fairest under Heaven's dome.

In every season the Old Well stands as Carolina's eternal symbolic center. It is particularly beautiful when April brings the brilliant pinks of dogwoods.

Alumni Hall appears to be adorned in a pink headdress and a fuscia-crocheted shawl this early April afternoon.

A random pattern of petals demonstrates that Nature's method of littering can sometimes bring pleasing, artistic results.

Chip Henderson

Dear Carolina Alumnus/Alumna:

What does Chapel Hill mean to you?

Chapel Hill is Franklin Street, Dean Smith, the Old Well, the Arboretum, Kenan Stadium and drop-add. For most of us it is all these and more. It's people. It's memories. It's the sights and sounds of the oldest and the most beautiful state university in this country.

Do you remember your first day of class, that first exam, the terror? Do you remember writing that 15-page essay on the role of Russia in the Crimean War, how the sun came up as you put the final words on page 14-and-a-half? When the old prof with the gray beard said your paper contained "remarkable insight"? Or the excitement that came as that special professor opened your eyes to ancient truths or made inert gasses come alive?

Do you remember standing in line to get tickets for a game in Carmichael? (Yes, I know some of you were waiting for a ball game in Woollen and others are still hoping to get into the new Smith Center.)

Things in Chapel Hill have changed for all of us. For some, it is disturbing to realize the Tin Can or our favorite tree may be no longer. Buildings that we don't recognize change the feel of a remembered favorite spot. Some of those special people who opened our eyes and ears to the world are no longer with us.

Wherever I go, Carolina alumni are always anxious to learn how things are in Chapel Hill. Many accuse me of living out a fantasy. I am. It is special to live in Chapel Hill, to work at UNC, to walk down Franklin Street and across the campus, to pass the Old Well, to see the excitement on the faces of students, to share the joys of Carmichael and now Smith Center moments, to sympathize over the anxieties of final exams, to revel in the anticipation of spring, and those beautiful dogwoods and azaleas.

I find what alumni care about most is not just buildings and places. They care about people, their classmates, their professors—even those who were tough but helped them find the way.

The pages that follow capture much of what makes the University special. Not only will you find breath-taking photographs of campus and Chapel Hill scenes, you'll also find nostalgic essays by many familiar and some unfamiliar Carolina alumni and friends.

We hope you'll cherish this exciting book and share it with your family and friends. If it causes you to renew your relationship with the University and your Alumni Association, naturally, we'll be pleased.

But, most of all, we hope the photos and essays that follow reassure you that as we approach the University's bicentennial, your alma mater remains committed to maintaining the traditions and values, beauty and buildings, ideas and ideals that make the University of North Carolina special.

Yours at Carolina,

Douglas S. Dibbert '70
Executive Director

East Building as drawn by student John Pettigrew in 1797.

NC Collection

THE UNIVERSITY IS BORN

1754 A full 39 years before the cornerstone was laid for Old East, the first state university building in the nation, North Carolina's people, led by acting Governor Matthew Rowan, petitioned for "the founding and endowing of a Public School" in the province. The problem they faced, of course, was that such a petition had to be approved by the Bishop of London and the King's Board of Trade. They received the answer they had expected: Permission denied.

1759 Still fuming, the North Carolina colonists would not give up the battle for a "Public School" of their own design. Governor Arthur Dobbs and the General Assembly again petitioned the King's Board of Trade, and once more their appeal was rejected.

1771 Governor William Tryon seems to have accurately assessed the politics of the "Public School" campaign: The King knew full-well that such a school would be run by Presbyterians, not Anglicans. Accordingly, Tryon fashioned a charter requiring that the president of the college be a member of the King's church. Surely, he thought, this would satisfy the Bishop and the Board of Trade.

Interestingly, if that petition had been granted it is likely that 150,000 of us today would be proudly telling our neighbors that the sky is a beautiful hue of "Queen's blue" and that Charlotte is "the Southern Side of Heaven." Tryon's petition, you see, was for "the founding and endowing of Queen's College in Mecklenburg County," not UNC-Chapel Hill.

1772 The King, of course, rejected the 1771 petition to charter Queen's College on the grounds that it would be a school for "Dissenters," i.e., Presbyterians. He was also equally outraged by the proposal to tax imported British liquor in order to fund the new school.

1773 Stubborn North Carolinians, vowing that they would not be denied their "Public School," knew now that they had to be discreet about its founding and operation. The trustees of Queen's College, therefore, illegally operated a school under the name "Queen's Museum."

1775 The colonists had had quite enough of British taxes on tea, paper, lead, molasses, and paint. On April 19 the Revolutionary War began at Lexington, Massachusetts.

1776 The war with the Mother Country was escalating, and on July 4 the colonists declared their independence from Great Britain. On October 15 the people of the new free state of North Carolina held an election to select delegates to a Provincial Congress "called for the express purpose of framing a Constitution."[1] At that Congress, which was held in November and December in Halifax, were four

1. R.D.W. Connor, *A Documentary History of the University of North Carolina, 1776-1799* (Chapel Hill: The University of North Carolina Press, 1953), Vol. I, p. 5.

former trustees of "Queen's Museum," including influential statesman Waightstill Avery of Mecklenburg.

On December 18 the North Carolina Congress ratified a new Constitution, at least part of which was borrowed from the Constitution which Pennsylvania had passed just a few weeks before.[2] That particular section, Article 41, foretold the eventual founding of the University of North Carolina: "That a School or Schools shall be established by the Legislature, for the convenient Instruction of Youth, with such Salaries to the Masters, paid by the public, as may enable them to instruct at low Prices; and all useful Learning shall be duely encouraged and promoted in one or more Universities."

1783
The Revolutionary War officially ended on September 3 with the signing of a peace treaty between the United States and Great Britain.

1784
Had he not been a man five years ahead of his time, perhaps a thousand Tar Heel romances might have been kindled lo these many years under the comforting boughs of the Sharpe Poplar. On November 8 William Sharpe, a Maryland-born Federalist from Rowan County, introduced a bill in the Legislature calling for the official chartering of "the North Carolina University." Of the defeat of the Sharpe bill, William Richardson Davie wrote: "The harried representatives were confronted with a multitude of claims and an empty till." There was no money for a university in war-torn North Carolina its charter would not come until Davie himself introduced a similar bill in 1789.

1789
On April 30 Federalist George Washington was inaugurated as the first President of the United States. Seven months later, on November 12, William R. Davie, a former student of Queen's Museum in Charlotte, introduced a bill in the legislature which would establish the University. Lest we overlook it, four days later North Carolina joined the Union as her twelfth state. Then, four weeks after it had been introduced, the Davie bill was passed. On December 11 the University was chartered, and on December 18 the Trustees held an unofficial, informal meeting in Fayetteville.[3]

Another war began. They must have had fighting blood in their veins, those hard-boiled founders of the state and the University. While money—or the lack of it—was a major topic at every early meeting of both the Trustees and the ever-watchful General Assembly, their gatherings were also filled with heated debates on Constitutional, moral and religious issues. While the war with Great Britain had officially ended in 1783, the battle over who would run the new country, the state and the University was just beginning to rage in 1789.

After the United States Constitution was hammered out, the Founding Fathers engaged in continuing debates over whether that document should be loosely interpreted, as was the view of George Washington, Alexander Hamilton, and the Federalist Party, or strictly interpreted, the philosophy embraced by Thomas Jefferson and the Republicans, often called the Democratic-Republicans. Washington and Hamilton called for a strong central government that would be undergirded by a national bank, they said. Jefferson, on the other hand, favored "states' rights" and "citizens' rights."

This philosophical struggle was brought to light in North Carolina when some state leaders questioned the true motivations and intentions of the University's founders. Some wondered if the school would evolve into a state-supported training ground for Federalists, led by William R. Davie himself.

The Funding Fathers. The University received its first major gift in 1789 when "Colonel Benjamin Smith offered. . . 20,000 acres of land,"[4] and even though the land was located in the wilds of Tennessee, the Trustees were jubilant. In 1790 the sum of $2,706.41 was received unexpectedly through the Clerk of Perquimans Court, and, as was required in the school's charter, the money was invested in United States stock.[5]

But funding did not come easy in those early years. A full two years after it was chartered, the University had a bank balance of $301.24 according to "a woeful financial report given by the Trustees."[5] That same month William R. Davie, in the face of stiff states' rights opposition, shepherded a bill through the General Assembly to grant a loan of $10,000 to the Trustees for the purpose of erecting buildings. Davie's bill squeaked by 57 to 53 in the House of Commons and 28 to 21 in the Senate. Of the Davie speech that day Judge Archibald Murphey later wrote, "I have the most vivid recollection of the greatness of his manner and the powers of his eloquence on that occasion." The loan, thanks to Davie's influence, was later converted into a gift.[7]

XL. That every Foreigner who comes to settle in this State, having first taken an Oath of Allegiance to the same, may purchase, or by other just Means acquire, hold and transfer, Land, or other real Estate; and after one Year's Residence, shall be deemed a free Citizen.

XLI. That a School or Schools shall be established by the Legislature, for the convenient Instruction of Youth, with such Salaries to the Masters, paid by the public, as may enable them to instruct at low Prices; and all useful Learning shall be duely encouraged and promoted in one or more Universities.

XLII. That no purchase of Lands shall be made of the *Indian* Natives, but on Behalf of the public, by Authority of the General Assembly.

XLIII. That the future Legislature of this State shall regulate Intails, in such a Manner as to prevent Perpetuities.

XLIV. That the Declaration of the Rights is hereby declared to be Part of the Constitution of this State, and ought never to be violated, on any Pretence whatsoever.

XLV. That any Member of either House of General Assembly shall have Liberty to dissent from, and protest against, any act or Resolve which he may think injurious to the Public, or any individual, and have the Reasons of his Dissent entered on the Journals.

XLVI. That neither House of the General Assembly shall proceed upon Public Business, unless a Majority of all the Members of such House are actually present; and that upon a Motion made and seconded, the Yeas and Nays upon any Question shall be taken and entered on the Journals; and that the Journals of the Proceedings of both Houses of the General Assembly shall be printed, and made public, immediately after their Adjournment.

† This Constitution is not intended to preclude the present Congress from making a temporary Provision for the well ordering of this State, until the General.....

NC Collection

Article XLI of the Constitution of 1776 called for "the establishment of ... one or more Universities" in North Carolina.

2. *Ibid,* p. 6.

3. William S. Powell, *The First State University* (Chapel Hill: The University of North Carolina Press, 1972), p. 5.

4. Kemp P. Battle, *History of the University of North Carolina* (Spartanburg, S.C.: The Reprint Company, Publishers, 1974, Vol. I, p. 13.

5. *Ibid,* p. 14.

6. *Ibid,* p. 16.

7. *Ibid,* p. 17.

The Founding Fathers. The list of the University's founders reads like a state geography lesson: Davie, Johnston, Iredell, Cabarrus, Graham, Person, Lenoir, Hargett, Stokes, Ashe, McDowell, Jones, Mebane, Martin, Kenan, Hoke, Avery, Haywood, Polk, Winston, Macon, and Moore. For some reason, though, the General Assembly's Name Selection Committee must have felt that no one would want to live in Hogg County or in Hoggsboro. Indeed, it was James Hogg "of Cross Creek (and later of Hillsborough) who was largely responsible for the choice of New Hope Chapel Hill as the site of the University. Hogg, a wealthy merchant and Trustee who served on the site selection committee, succeeded in persuading some of his Orange County friends to contribute land and money for the new school."[8] These gifts—from Messrs. Hogan, Mark Morgan, Yergan, McCauley, Pipers, Craig, Barbee, Jones, Hardy Morgan, and Daniel—totaled 1,380 acres and cash of £798.[9]

If University athletes of the 20th century would play basketball in "Blue Heaven," then surely the school's first gymnasium should have been dubbed "Hogg Heaven." At the very least the cafeteria should have been named Hogg Hall since William Lenoir already had both a town *and* a county named for him.

1793

The minutes from an early meeting of the Trustees show that James Patterson of Chatham County received a contract "for erecting a two-storied brick building (Old East), 96 feet 7 inches long and 40 feet 1½ inches wide, for $5,000, the University to furnish the brick, sash weights, locks, hooks, fastenings and painting. The building was to contain 16 rooms with four passages, and to be finished by the first of November, 1794. The cornerstone was laid on the 12th of October, 1793 (University Day), and on the same day the lots in the village were sold for 1,534 pounds ($3,168), payable in one and two years, good security being given. It was thought that 'the amount of the sales furnishes a pleasing and undeniable proof of the high estimation in which the beautiful spot is held.' A four-acre lot was reserved for the building of a residence for the President."[10]

1794

The Trustees decided that the University should open its doors on January 15, 1795, and that tuition prices should be established as follows: "Reading, writing, arithmetic and bookkeeping for all or any of them eight Dollars per Annum. The Latin, Greek, and French languages, the English Grammar, Geography, History and the Belles Letters, for all or any of them twelve and a half Dollars. Geometry with its practical branches Astronomy, natural and moral Philosophy, Chemistry, and the principles of Agriculture for all or any of them fifteen Dollars provided that no Student shall pay more than 15 Dollars per Annum for his tuition let him be taught what he may."[11] The President, it was decided, "shall have the... use of the President's House; be styled the Professor of Humanity; receive a salary of three hundred Dollars from the Treasurer of the Board; and in addition to that sum shall be entitled to have and receive to his own use two-thirds of all tuition monies."[12]

The Board appointed a committee (Messrs. Lenoir, Stone, Lane, Porter and Haywood) "to report the quantity and quality of the meats and drinks to be furnished to students. The diet recommended: For breakfast—Coffee and tea, or chocolate and tea, one warm roll, one loaf of wheat or corn flour, at the option of the student, with a sufficiency of butter; For dinner—A dish or cover of bacon and greens, or beef and turnips, together with a sufficient quantity of fresh meats, or fowls, or pudding and tarts, with a sufficiency of wheat and corn bread; For supper—Coffee, tea, or milk at the option of the Steward, with the necessary quantity of bread or biscuit."[13] The committee added that the Steward was expected to furnish a clean table cloth every other day.[14]

1795

Battle's writings tell us that on January 15 the University opened, as scheduled, but that Presiding Professor Dr. David Ker had no one to teach. "It was not until February 12 that Hinton James arrived from Wilmington, with no companion. For two weeks, in his loneliness, he constituted the entire student body."[15]

8. Powell, *op. cit.,* p. 9.

9. Minutes of the UNC Board of Trustees, December 3-13, 1792.

10. Battle, *op. cit.,* p. 34.

11. Connor, *op. cit.,* pp. 268-269.

12. *Ibid,* p. 269.

13. Battle, *op. cit.,* pp. 51.

14. *Ibid,* p. 51.

15. *Ibid,* p. 63.

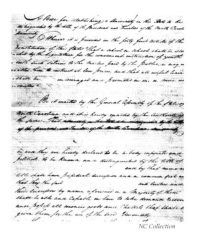

NC Collection

With these words William Sharpe of Rowan introduced his 1784 bill which would have established the University: "It is the indispensable duty of every Legislature to consult the happiness of a rising generation." The State had an empty treasury at that time, and Sharpe's bill was defeated.

William R. Davie, the Father of the University

WILLIAM R. DAVIE AND THE FOUNDING FATHERS

Adapted from the writings of Kemp P. Battle[16]

In the month of November, 1789, our State, after a hesitation of a year, entered the American Union. In the month of December, as if forming a part of a comprehensive plan, the charter of the University, under the powerful advocacy of William R. Davie, was granted by the General Assembly. The Trustees under the charter comprised great men of the State, good men of the State, trusted leaders of the people.

The chairman was Governor Samuel Johnston, a man of wise conservatism. There were James Iredell, one of the earliest Judges of the Supreme Court of the United States, and Alfred Moore, his successor in this high office. There were the first Federal District Judge, Colonel John Stokes, and John Sitgreaves, his successor.

There were three signers of the Constitution of the United States: Hugh Williamson, the historian, William Blount, afterwards a U.S. Senator from Tennessee, and Richard Dobbs Spaight, who later served as delegate to the Congress of the Confederation, and of the United States, and as Governor of North Carolina.

Of others destined to be Governors, there were Samuel Ashe, then Judge, Benjamin Williams, and the first benefactor of the University, Benjamin Smith, and William Richardson Davie, its father.

There were military men who had been conspicuous fighters in the Revolution: General Joseph Graham, scarred with wounds in the defense of Charlotte under Davie; General Thomas Person, William Lenoir, Joseph McDowell, and Joseph Dixon (or Dickson), men who were active in thwarting the plans of Cornwallis; and Henry William Harrington, a militia general.

Of the State judiciary we find three judges—Samuel Spencer, John Williams, and Samuel Ashe, already mentioned. Other distinguished Trustees included Archibald McLaine, Willie Jones, Stephen Cabarrus, long Speaker of the House of Commons, and John Haywood,

Benjamin Smith gave 20,000 acres of Tennessee land to the University in 1789, and he later served the school as both President and Trustee.

Archibald Murphey, class of 1799, served as an instructor and a Trustee, and his call for a library and for funding for classroom equipment led to many progressive changes during his 33-year association with the University.

William A. Graham, class of 1824, served as governor, U.S. Navy Secretary, and UNC Trustee.

popular State Treasurer for 40 years. There were the State's first two U.S. Senators—Samuel Johnston and Benjamin Hawkins; Charles Johnson, then Speaker of the State Senate; James Holland of Guilford; Alexander Mebane of Orange; Joseph Winston of Surry; William Barry Grove of Cumberland; John Hay of Fayetteville; James Hogg, an enlightened merchant of Fayetteville and Hillsborough; Adlai Osborne, the highly esteemed Clerk of Rowan Superior Court; eminent teacher Rev. Samuel McCorkle, D.D.; State Senators Frederick Hargett, Robert Snead, Joel Lane and John Macon; and House of Commons members Nathaniel Macon, John Hamilton, William Porter and Robert Dickson.

Richard Dobbs Spaight served as North Carolina's Governor when the University opened its doors in 1795. He served the school as Trustee, fund-raiser, architect, and benefactor.

The moving spirit of this distinguished band was William Richardson Davie. No common man, he had been a gallant cavalry officer in the Revolution—a strong staff on which General Greene had leaned. Davie had been conspicuous in civil pursuits, an able lawyer and an orator of wide influence. With Washington, Madison and other great men, he had assisted in evolving the grandest government of all ages, the American Union, out of an ill-governed and disintegrated confederacy. He was beyond his times in the advocacy of a broad, generous education.

Judge Archibald Murphey had this to say of Davie: "He was a tall, elegant man in his person, graceful and commanding in his manners. His voice was mellow, and adapted to the expression of every passion; his style was magnificent and flowing; he had a greatness of manner in public speaking which suited his style, and gave to his speeches an imposing effect. He was a laborious student, arranged his discourses with care, and where the subject merited his genius, poured forth a torrent of eloquence that astonished and enraptured his audience."

Davie drew for the University the "Plan of Studies" pursued for many years, and maintained its interest by his purse, his eloquence, his counsels, and constant attention to its exercises. The Dialectic Society is the fortunate owner of an excellent portrait of this great man—the picture of a man of military bearing, strikingly handsome, a gentleman, a scholar and a statesman.

16. *Ibid*, pp. 3-5.

James Knox Polk, class of 1818, served as President of the United States from 1845 to 1849. Born in Mecklenburg County near Charlotte, Polk credited his training in UNC's Dialectic Society as a major factor in his political success story.

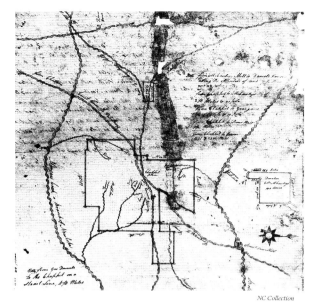

Site map of the University as drawn by surveyor John Daniel in 1792.

HOW FIRM THE FOUNDATION

by Sam J. Ervin, Jr.

In the late fall of 1792, while King George still sat on his throne—wondering how he had lost the colonies—a half-dozen men rode their horses up a wooded ridge in the middle of North Carolina. They were greeted by a handful of farmers who, like themselves, had won a dream of independence and now sought another dream. They wanted a good education for their children.

The men on horseback had spent a week searching for a site to locate the University that would supply this education. The farmers offered them money, land and bricks. "Build here," they said, "on New Hope Chapel Hill." A year later a delegation of state officials gathered there and gently lowered a cornerstone into the red Orange clay—gently, for they knew they were dropping a pebble into a vast, mirror-smooth lake.

Fifteen months later, on January 15, 1795, Governor Richard Dobbs Spaight and a group of dignitaries and Chapel Hill farmers gathered for the official opening of the University. Predictably, it rained. Just as predictably, the first student—Hinton James of Wilmington—was late for class by four weeks.

The debating societies were the heart of the University for nearly 120 years. They supplied the foundation of virtually every important institution you now find at Chapel Hill—the University departments, the library, student government, and the various professional and literary societies. More men went out for debating than football, and no society member ever broke his leg speaking in public. President James K. Polk was a society member, and he told the audience at the 1847 commencement that those debates had trained him to preside over the United States' government.

Public opinion during this time judged the success of the University more by the number of students enrolled than the number of Latin works the students could translate. The diploma presented each graduate did not signify scholarship so much as the ability to manage other men, and in this sense, the 800,000 residents of North Carolina had good cause to be satisfied.

In its first century the University produced a U.S. President and Vice President and literally dozens of Congressmen and cabinet members, foreign ministers, clergymen, and civic leaders, and every one of them could translate the Latin inscriptions on his diploma.

After we graduate and go our separate ways, we spend the rest of our lives repeating to our friends and families all of our fond memories from Chapel Hill. We fix the time spent here in a special section of our minds, and so—in effect—we never leave; we can always come home again. And when we do come home—for a ballgame, a reunion, to watch a son or daughter graduate, or just by chance—we wander nostalgically down the old brick paths, across the still, green grasses, beneath the poplars and along the stone walls, and whisper to one another that we don't recognize the place.

Sam J. Ervin, Jr.

The steps to Wilson Library lead to many open doors.

Chip Henderson

*Zebulon B. Vance—UNC student, Civil War Governor of
North Carolina, and financial contributor in time of need.*

UNIVERSITY MEN IN THE CONFEDERACY

by Dr. Archie K. Davis

The people of North Carolina were strongly divided on the question of secession. In a statewide referendum held on 28 February 1861, after seven southern states had already joined the Confederacy, a majority of North Carolina citizens voted against calling a convention to even consider the question. It was not until 15 April that the die was cast. On that day Simon Cameron, Secretary of War, wired Governor John W. Ellis to provide "two (2) Regiments of Military for immediate Service." The Governor's response was prompt and to the point: "You can get no troops from North Carolina." It was not until 20 May that the state formally withdrew from the Union.

In the light of her reluctant withdrawal, it is ironic that North Carolina should have suffered more than did any other state in the Confederacy during the four, long years of bitter warfare. Nor did any other state university in the South quite match the contributions made by the University of North Carolina in terms of manpower and leadership. Yet the University was the only educational institution of collegiate rank in the South which did not fail to hold commencement exercises every year during the war—even for the one remaining member of the senior class of 1865, whose poor health disqualified him from military service. In fact, the doors of the University never closed during the war and "the old college bell was rung daily and prayers were said in the chapel."

Although the state was reluctant to leave the Union, the "University men" responded swiftly to the call to arms. The senior class of 1861 left school before receiving their diplomas at commencement. Of the 80 members of the freshman class of 1861, only one would remain long enough to graduate. It is not surprising, therefore, that the student body enrollment dropped dramatically from 430 to 63 within the first two years of the war. Before war's end, one-third of the faculty would volunteer for service. Of the 2,592 men who matriculated at the University from 1830 to 1867, and who were living in 1861, a total of 1,062, or 40.9 percent, entered the armies of the Confederacy. Of this number, 312, or 34 percent, lost their lives. Among the 1,331 younger alumni who matriculated between 1851 and 1860, inclusive, 749, or 56.2 percent, entered service.

But the contributions of the "University men" were obviously not limited to the military. In the state legislature, in the Confederate Congress, in the administrative branches of both governments, and abroad, they played a distinctive and vital leadership role, but none more so than in the administration of their own state government. The three war governors of North Carolina—John W. Ellis, Henry Toole Clark, and Zebulon Baird Vance—provided a sequential leadership of unparalleled vitality and strength, resulting in a Herculean response to the mounting needs of the Confederacy. As Dr. R.D.W. Connor once wrote, "To these three 'University men' more than to any others it is due that North Carolina sent into the Confederate armies more soldiers than she had voters; that she furnished about one-fifth of all the troops of the Confederacy; that her troops were better clothed, better armed, and better equipped than those of any other Confederate state."

As for the approximately 140,000 Confederates who died of wounds or disease while in service, there were 42,000 North Carolinians who never came home—an appalling mortality rate. Of the 40 North Carolina regiments which sustained the heaviest losses during the war, 18 were commanded by "University men." And, Dr. Connor reminds us, the spirit of these men seemingly manifested itself on every major field of battle. For example, C.M. Avery (class of 1839), in leading the 33rd North Carolina at Chancellorsville, sustained a loss of 41.4 percent; George Burgwyn Anderson (a matriculate of 1848), commanded the 4th North Carolina at Seven Pines, with a loss of 54 percent; and Robert H. Cowan (class of 1844) was in command of the 18th North Carolina during the Seven Days' battles, with a loss of 56.5 percent. It was James Johnston Pettigrew, first honor man of 1847, who commanded the North Carolina troops in the famous Pettigrew-Pickett charge on the third day at Gettysburg, and Bryan Grimes, also a "University man," who planned the last battle and led the last charge at Appomattox. It is little wonder that North Carolina could later claim to have been "First at Bethel, Farthest to the front at Gettysburg and Chickamauga, and Last at Appomattox."

The last words of two "University men" who died at Gettysburg will forever serve as a poignant reminder of that nobility of spirit which conquers even in death. Their names were Isaac E. Avery and Henry King (Harry) Burgwyn, and both were regimental commanders. Colonel Avery, a classmate of Pettigrew, was struck down as he led Hoke's brigade across an open field against a strongly posted enemy. He lived just long enough to scrawl on the back of a crumpled envelope, "Major, tell my father I died with my face to the enemy." This old envelope survives to this day. A more sublime or more meaningful epitaph has never been written.

Colonel Harry Burgwyn, class of 1859, was shot down on the afternoon of the first day at Gettysburg as he led the 26th North Carolina up the bloody slopes of McPherson's Woods (now Reynolds' Grove). This gallant regiment of Pettigrew's brigade gained lasting fame by crushing Meredith's Iron Brigade and forcing the Federals to fall back on Cemetery Ridge. In perhaps less than an hour of fierce combat, 588 of Burgwyn's men were killed or wounded out of 800 engaged. As he lay dying, he was heard to exclaim: "I know my gallant regiment will do their duty—where is my sword. . . ?" Prophetic were his last words. On the afternoon of the third day barely 200 men of the 26th could be mustered for the great Pettigrew-Pickett charge. A remnant of the 26th reached the "high stone wall" on Cemetery Ridge, truly the high water mark of the Confederacy, only to be literally blown away by an artillery blast of double canister from a distance of less than fifteen paces. Barely seventy men were able to retrace their steps over the frightful 1,400 yards to the west that lay between them and some degree of safety behind Seminary Ridge.

Within a period of forty-eight hours, at least 708 out of 800 engaged were killed, wounded or missing. Of the thirty-nine officers, thirty-four were killed or wounded. Of the seventeen men who served in the color guard, including volunteers, seven were killed and ten wounded. According to Colonel William F. Fox, a noted authority on Civil War casualties, the 26th sustained the heaviest loss of any regiment on either side in any battle during the entire war. He later wrote: "I am inclined to believe that in time this regiment [the 26th] will become as well known in history as the Light Brigade at Balaklava."

And certainly, throughout the war, "University men" from all walks of life made a magnificent contribution to the noble effort of their beloved state.

Eleanor Swain had a charm that could melt the heart of the coldest Yankee brigadier.

ELEANOR AND THE BRIGADIER

by Maggie Palmer Lauterer

The tintype photographs that have survived the 120-odd years since the ill-fated war of Southern Liberation tell part of this tale of love and hate.

There is a tintype of Eleanor. She was a darkhaired girl. Sometimes she would pull her locks back with a ribbon and allow only a tiny curl to escape at the edges of her forehead. She wore a dress cut fashionably below the shoulder blades, made of a light fabric, probably pink, laced in black. She chose to wear a string of carved black beads.

Some would say her face was solemn, pretty but not beautiful, with large, dark eyes. Her lips were full and feminine, but decidedly set. There was a no-nonsense look to the young Eleanor Swain.

Eleanor's father was University President David Swain, the man called "Old Bunc" by his students because he had been born in a log cabin in Western North Carolina's Buncombe County. He had served three terms as Governor of North Carolina before becoming President of the University in 1835. He had an uphill battle to fight, not having an academic background. Though he had his law degree, many of the faculty openly criticized his lack of a liberal education, but he proved himself a worthy leader. It was he who directed William Battle to organize the law school, it was he who planted trees across the campus, and it was his project to have the campus rocks gathered together to build rock walls along the old campus boundaries. Many of those walls stand today.

But it was the war that brought the most difficult period of his presidency—those tumultuous years when Swain struggled to keep the doors of the University open. All the young southern men had dressed in gray and marched away, leaving only faculty members too old to fight and a few students who were unable to bear arms. Through the war years the University remained open, but only as a pale shadow of what it had been.

The spring of 1865 was a tense time for Chapel Hill. The noble cause for which so many had fought and died was faltering. General William Tecumseh Sherman had defeated General Joseph E. Johnston at Bentonville, and Union troops were marching toward Raleigh. Confederate troops under the command of General Joseph Wheeler moved into Chapel Hill to protect the town and the University.

Governor Zebulon Baird Vance, a former student of Swain's at the University and a fellow Buncombe Countian, requested that President Swain and former Governor Graham take a message of peace to Sherman before he reached Raleigh. In a conference held 14 miles outside the capital, Swain brought assurances that North Carolina no longer posed a threat, and Sherman promised protection for Raleigh and the University.

Swain was waiting on the Capitol steps when the Union troops arrived, and he watched as the United States flag was raised where the Confederate flag had flown. The next morning, a Union force of 4,000 men marched into Chapel Hill. Leading the troops was their commander, 30-year-old Brigadier General Smith D. Atkins of Freeport, Illinois.

The residents of Chapel Hill had prepared for the worst. They had hidden their silver in wells, hidden paintings between walls, and buried their jewelry. Nervous faculty members had removed the lenses of the University's telescopes and hidden their watches and jewelry in the tubes of the instruments.

President Swain received General Atkins in his library. The University's President was determined to have a peaceful transition and to keep the University and its grounds intact during the occupation. In the course of conversation the two men discovered a mutual interest in American history. Swain told Atkins that he owned an order book that had once belonged to Lord Cornwallis, and he summoned his daughter Eleanor to bring the book.

The attraction between the young Eleanor and Smith Atkins was immediate, and small towns being what they are, their courtship was soon public knowledge. They shared company openly and properly, but many residents of Chapel Hill, still tasting the bitter gall of defeat, were appalled.

The Union Army's band held concerts "to compliment President Swain, who had been cooperative in all matters of the occupations." Then General Atkins gave a fine horse to the University President and another one to Eleanor. "Stolen," some Chapel Hillians said. "Stolen from some Southern family."

Tempers flared at the courtship, and when General Atkins led his troops out of town in early May, the Swains hoped that Eleanor would lose interest in her "Yankee lover." But the couple continued to correspond frequently and decided to be married in August.

With such ill feelings in the community, the Swains tried to persuade their daughter not to marry. But she stood firm, and her parents decided to stand behind her. Invitations were issued, only to be thrown angrily to the ground. Many of those who acknowledged the announcements refused to attend.

The wedding, held at the Swain's home on August 23, was attended by only a few friends. University students disrupted the festivities by ringing the college bell throughout the ceremony and reception. They later hanged both Swain and General Atkins in effigy.

Soon after the wedding the couple left by horse and buggy for Illinois, but President Swain stayed to face the wrath of the community.

Swain also suffered through the days of Reconstruction that followed the war, and the man who had fought so hard to keep open the doors of the University presided over the closing of the University in 1868. A few weeks later, Swain died of injuries he received in a buggy accident.

You can look for Swain these days and find him still in a few places. His portrait hangs in the Morehead Planetarium, and Swain Hall is named for him. The old cabin associated with his name still stands on the northern slopes of the Beaverdam Valley near Asheville. And his name graces the pages of a few history books. Perhaps his greatest contribution to the University's history was this: He stood up for his beliefs. That is a legacy which has been passed down to us through many fine successors to Swain and through thousands of faithful, undaunted faculty members. That is worth remembering now and then as we hurry past Swain's rock walls on our way across campus.

Joseph Caldwell—faithful President, professor and Trustee. NC Collection

CURRICULUM, CONFLICT AND CONTROVERSY, 1795-1885

Adapted from the writings of Louis Round Wilson[17]

From the day it opened the University's curriculum reflected the two points of view held by Trustees William R. Davie and Rev. Samuel E. McCorkle. Davie proposed the practical subjects of English and mathematics, ancient history, the chemistry of agriculture and other related sciences, and modern language. McCorkle, a Presbyterian minister and highly successful teacher was, like Davie, a graduate of Princeton. Drawing upon his experience as a teacher, he favored the classical program of the times in which Latin and Greek were fundamental. He also included moral philosophy, English, mathematics, and ancient history. The resulting combination of the two plans was to be directed by a Presiding Professor (1795-1804) or President (after 1804) who also served as Professor of Humanities, thus assuming the conduct of the institution in accord with the broad concept embodied in that term.

For the first nine years the University was directed by a succession of four Presiding Professors, assisted by tutors. The first was David Ker (Trinity College, Dublin), followed by Charles W. Harris (Princeton), Joseph Caldwell (Princeton) and James Gillaspie. The Trustees reserved the title of President until Joseph Caldwell had demonstrated his ability to fill the position in accord with the importance which the Trustees attached to the office.

Following the appointment of Caldwell, first as Presiding Professor (1796-97 and again in 1799) and then as President in 1804, the curriculum underwent modification. Davie moved to South Carolina in 1805, and consequently the classical concept became more generally adopted, with Latin and Greek both required for a degree. When Professors Elisha Mitchell (for whom Mount Mitchell is named) and Dennison L. Olmsted, both graduates of Yale, joined the staff in 1817-18, a place was made in the curriculum for additional subjects such as calculus, chemistry, geology, and minerology.

But the curriculum was only one matter to demand Caldwell's attention. The faculty had to administer discipline. The Trustees had enacted a long list of regulations for the young boys who attended the University's grammar school; these rules were considered onerous by older students, and friction developed. In 1799 a serious riot occurred in which several tutors were attacked by students. This occasioned controversy over the University,

David L. Swain—University student, Governor of North Carolina, Trustee and President of UNC, father of Eleanor Swain, and campus beautification architect. Elisha Mitchell, for whom the highest mountain east of the Mississippi River is named, was both a revered professor and the man most credited for UNC's beautiful rock walls and stately grounds.

which at that early date was charged with being "aristocratic"; the students were called "immoral" and "resistant to discipline." Caldwell came to the University's defense in letters to the press.

In the administration of discipline the faculty had to discover and apprehend the rule breakers, try them, and punish them. Caldwell was reputed to be fleet of foot, and thus the President himself frequently played the role of "apprehending officer." The riot in 1798-99 resulted in the expulsion of a number of the advanced students, and consequently only three seniors graduated that year.

Robert H. Chapman served as President from 1812 to 1816, but he was subjected to such indignities by the students that he resigned. Caldwell again assumed the presidency, and by 1822 he had found time to publish a textbook in geometry. He was also interested in astronomical observations, and in 1832 he established the first observatory to be built by a U.S. college or university.

Caldwell received authorization and funding from the Trustees to take a ten-month trip to Europe (1824-25) for the purpose of purchasing books for the library, astronomical apparatus, and a cabinet of mineral specimens for use in the study of geology and other scientific subjects. Upon his return to Chapel Hill he was met by a large group of students, faculty, and residents and given a tremendous ovation.

Governor David L. Swain served as University President for a remarkable 33 years (1835-68), and as a result of his emphasis on an increased enrollment, UNC's student body of 461 ranked second in size only to Yale's in 1858. During his administration Swain contributed to the school's development by chartering the Historical Society; establishing the North Carolina *Magazine;* establishing the School of Law (1845); enclosing the campus within attractive rock walls; planting many beautiful shrubs and rose bushes; and by overseeing the construction of Smith Hall, New East and New West.

The highly-controversial marriage of Swain's daughter to a Yankee brigadier at the end of the Civil War helped lead to the termination of Swain's administration in 1868. Two months after his shocking dismissal, Swain went driving with Professor Fetter in a buggy drawn by a spirited horse given him by none other than General William T. Sherman. The horse became frightened, ran away, overturned the buggy and threw out both the occupants. Professor Fetter recovered quickly, but President Swain died some 18 days later.

Swain had not been the only leader dismissed in 1868 by hostile Governor W.W. Holden and the Trustees; indeed, the entire faculty was fired. Holden's plans failed miserably, and by 1871 the University had to close for lack of students. Holden himself was impeached, tried, convicted and dismissed from office by the General Assembly. Tradition has it that one student chalked these words on a blackboard as the doors were being locked: "This old University has busted and gone to hell today."

In 1875 a revitalized General Assembly, drawn in part from former friends of the school, provided for a new Board of Trustees and annual financial support of $7,500. The University reopened, and in 1876 Kemp P. Battle began his distinguished 16-year term as President. Battle, a graduate and former tutor of the University, a lawyer and former State Treasurer, initially concerned himself with reducing the tensions and animosities engendered by the Civil War and Reconstruction. Once a new faculty was in place and student life had settled, Battle established a workable system of student self-government; organized a program of graduate studies; established a summer school for the training of public school teachers—the first in the nation to cover the entire curriculum; established Schools of Medicine and Pharmacy (1879); secured an appropriation for maintenance from the General Assembly (1881); and made great improvements to the school's library.

In 1885 the Trustees passed a regulation barring the use of University facilities for dancing, a recreational activity which was not popular with many alumni and friends of the school. Battle succeeded in having a private citizen purchase a lot adjoining University property, on which was erected a dance hall which the University later rented for use as a gymnasium.

17. Louis Round Wilson, *Historical Sketches* (Durham: Moore Publishing Company, 1976), pp. 11-24.

The faculty of the University, 1887, led by President Battle (front row, holding a cane).

THE 1880's

Adapted from the writings of Kemp P. Battle[18] and Louis R. Wilson[19]

President Battle clearly understood the principle that, no matter what he might do to try to prevent it, sooner or later the young men in his charge were going to act like "college boys." One Saturday night following a lecture by a distinguished guest, Battle and the visitor were disturbed from their sleep "by the sounds of. . . continuous bell ringing. I politely sent word to the perpetrators to please discontinue the noise, but my request went unheeded. Finally, at three o'clock in the morning, my patience was exhausted. I went to the South Building and found that the 'rioters' had pushed a cow up to the third story and tied her horns to the rope of the school's bell!'

In 1884 a Visiting Committee "composed of able and practical men headed by Honorable A. Haywood Merritt from Chatham" prepared a report on "the State of the University." Included in their report were the following observations: "Your committee sincerely assures the parents of boys at the University that there is a very healthy moral and religious atmosphere here. We are assured of this by personal observation of the students in the recitation rooms, in their private apartments (dormitory rooms), in the Campus, at the meals and at their daily worship in the College Chapel. On the Sabbath the village churches are open to and attended by the students; and each student is expected to attend one of the four Bible classes, conducted by the Faculty for their benefit. There is no such thing as 'deviling the Faculty,' and cheating on recitation or examination is not tolerated by the students themselves. Hazing the Fresh (freshmen) is also under ban.

"On the matter of expenses, we are assured that the total expenses for tuition, books, board, fuel, lights and washing need not exceed $200 per year. Considering its advantages, the University is one of the very cheapest institutions in the land.

The original Memorial Hall, dedicated in 1885, cost approximately $45,000 to construct.

"As for the University Library, it numbers nine thousand volumes and two thousand pamphlets. Many of these books are exceedingly rare and valuable, but are so arranged as to be comparatively useless for consultation. Some of them are on shelves twelve or fifteen feet from the floor. With nothing but a frail ladder to aid one in reaching them, the sublime ascent is likely to end in a ridiculous descent."

Battle had to contend with a distinct shortage of both space and capital, for in a University President's life there is rarely an abundance of either. Writing about the 1883 Commencement, he said: "I was sitting by Governor Thomas J. Jarvis on the rostrum in Gerrard Hall, which was filled to its utmost capacity. Looking out of the doors and windows we could see at least one-third more of good citizens unable to enter the Hall. I said, 'Governor, if you will promise the people that next year we will have a building large enough to accommodate everybody, I will show you where the money will come from.' With great applause he made the promise." Governor Jarvis "secured, on extremely favorable terms, bricks made at the State Penitentiary," Battle found the money, and Gerrard Hall was expanded. But additional space was still desperately needed.

The original Memorial Hall, which according to the architect's estimates was to cost $20,000, was completed in 1885. "Its final cost was $45,000," said Battle, "so it is evident that the architect, who died before its completion, either was ignorant of the art of estimating cost, or, which is more likely, he planned with no regard for expense, trusting that the Trustees would be too proud to have an unfinished building on their hands." Originally begun as a tribute to President David L. Swain, the building became "Memorial Hall" when Battle recognized that more funds could be raised if families of deceased alumni would be approached about making appropriate memorial gifts to the school, with marble tablets as tributes to the deceased leaders and veterans. Battle's fundraising effort, along with a generous $8,000 loan (later converted to a gift) from Paul C. Cameron, led to the completion of one of the most "interesting" buildings ever erected in the state.

Louis Round Wilson called the original Memorial Hall (on Cameron Avenue) "a giant, turtle-shaped monster which defied description . . . a towering elephant with unprecedented height, width and length, equipped with amazingly hard seats." It was dedicated at Commencement, 1885, before a faculty of nine, graduates numbering 26, and perhaps as many as 2,000 family members and friends. Right Reverend A.W. Wilson delivered the dedication sermon, reminding the audience that "without God's aid, all our intellectual labor is worthless."

Battle later admitted that the acoustics in Memorial Hall were "not good, and that on certain benches the reverberation of the speaker's voice is painfully apparent." The building, which also served as a gymnasium, was later found to be structurally unsafe, and in 1930 it was razed and replaced on the same site by a new Memorial Hall.[20] "Since funds for seats were not available, the uncomfortable old heart-pine benches from the old building were installed in the new building."[21]

Based on their oath that "members would not use intoxicating liquors at any banquet given at Chapel Hill," fraternities were "granted admission" in 1885. "Water closets were introduced in 1887, and hygiene lectures were given twice a week. It was resolved to heat the chapel (Gerrard Hall) when used for preaching or other services. And, in the same year, the library grew to 20,000 volumes, and the student body totalled 200."

On June 5, 1889, "a large body of alumni, Trustees, Faculty and invited guests from Harvard, Yale and many other universities assembled in Gerrard Hall to partake of an elaborate banquet in honor of the University's centennial anniversary. The Honorable Walter L. Steele, President of the Alumni Association, gave the introductory address. After surveying the vast numbers of distinguished guests—many of whom would no doubt give lengthy toasts that would extend well into the night—Steele quoted Daniel Webster: "Ye solid men of Boston, make no long orations!"

18. Battle, *op. cit.,* Vol. II, pp. 193-443.
19. Wilson, *op. cit.,* pp. 21-24.
20. Powell, *op. cit.,* p. 105.
21. *Ibid,* p. 193.

The Chapel Hill Post Office, 1892.

The original Tar Heel, *born in 1893, was designed as a puff sheet for University athletics.*

THE 1890's

Adapted from the writings of Kemp P. Battle[22] *and Louis R. Wilson*[23]

In 1891 "a small, wooden infirmary was erected; it had three well-furnished rooms." George T. Winston became the University's President that year. He was hailed by Battle as a "distinguished student and enlightened Professor of Latin and German, a man of boundless energy, vigorous health, and a bold spirit which feared nothing and was appalled by no obstacles. . . a fluent and strong speaker who loved the University. . . . Confronted with the difficulty of the students of the post-war period to meet the cost of a college education, Winston waged a vigorous campaign to secure endowments for tuition scholarships and to bring the enrollment of the University back up to nearly its pre-war number, and in both efforts he was remarkably successful."

Because of his keen interest in public and secondary schools, Winston was active in organizing the North Carolina Teachers Association and the Southern Association of Secondary Schools and Colleges.

Battle wrote that his successor "used skillful detective work in securing the conviction of a whiskey dealer, a man who had repeatedly broken the law by selling spirits within four miles of University buildings." To do so Winston had to appear before a U.S. Court in Greensboro. And in 1893 he led the fight to defeat a Davidson College-backed bill in the General Assembly which in many respects could have turned the University into a graduate school, forbidden by law to teach undergraduate courses offered at other institutions in the state.

On Washington's Birthday, 1892, "the students assembled to carry out the annual buffoonery of granting medals to Freshmen. They were given in pure fun, intended and understood as such. Hawkins, Pruden and Rogers tied for the ugly man's medal, Horn won the 'dude's medal,' Weil—without opposition—was selected most boring, and Morris won the fool's medal. Welsh won the medal for 'general cussedness,' Shelton for 'blusher,' and Buck Guthrie was unanimously voted the 'Liar's Medal,' even though he was a Sophomore."

In an 1894 article entitled "The Expansion of the University," Winston wrote that "enrollment has increased from 198 in 1890 to 446 in 1894, the highest before the war being 463. Three new departments have been added: History, Biology and Pedagogics." Winston went on to address the subject of "University Spirit": "The aim of the University is to develop men. It teaches how to think. It knows that a man must find truth for himself if he would really comprehend it. The University is distinctly Christian in its moral standards. It seeks to promote character, righteousness and holiness rather than to emphasize doctrines. It aims to make good citizens, not partisans. It teaches men to love the truth and have respect for others who love the truth. The University is a sort of miniature State, a little world whose members, representing every condition of wealth and poverty, every type of local character, every phase of religious faith and political belief, combine to produce not only a strong resultant of mental, moral, and physical forces, but also a safe and well-balanced standard of manhood."

Winston also addressed the subject of athletics: "The college Hercules of today. . . finds his glory in the ballground . . . where in 90 minutes he works off two to eight pounds of vice, idleness, and corruption—

The South Building and the New Well in 1892.

The Glee Club, 1892.

commonly known as fat. It would be dishonest not to say that the greatest force in the University contributing to sobriety, manliness, healthfulness, and morality generally, is athletics."

In his last presidential report (1896) Winston reported that "some immorality and rowdyism had exhibited themselves during the fall term. The Faculty will endeavor to prevent a recurrence of these evils by excluding from the University those students whose chief interest is not in their studies; excluding from membership in football and baseball teams those who neglect their studies or are on probation for immorality; and requiring that team members pledge themselves not to drink or gamble during their trips."

Edwin A. Alderman became President of the University in 1896. He had been superintendent of the Goldsboro public schools, a member of the faculty of what is now UNC-G, and a History and Philosophy of Education Professor at UNC. Battle called him "an arduous and successful laborer for the teachers and the children of our public schools." Alderman's accomplishments included the reestablishment of the summer school program and the School of Pharmacy; the admission of women to the University as upper classpersons; the completion of Carr Dormitory; and the establishment of a school-wide water system.

In 1897 Mary MacRae became the first woman to register as a UNC student, but the distinction of being the first female *graduate* went to Sallie W. Stockard, class of '98.[24]

22. Battle, *op. cit.,* pp. 444-571.
23. Wilson, *op. cit.,* pp. 24-29.
24. Powell, *op. cit.,* pp. 130 and 140.

Mary MacRae and the Tar Heel *staff of 1898.*

*Many a student has taken these steps in
old Bingham Hall three at a time in order
to be punctual for an English or history class.*

*University Lake, the area's source of drink-
ing water, is a serene retreat for sailing
teams and students seeking a quiet place.*

President Kemp Plummer Battle

Louis Round Wilson

1900-1930: A COLLEGE BECOMES A UNIVERSITY

Adapted from the writings of Louis Round Wilson[25]

The period from 1900 to 1930 was a time when this institution made the change from an excellent liberal arts college with three professional schools more or less loosely connected with it to a full-fledged, mature university still engaged in teaching undergraduates, but likewise devoted to study at the graduate and professional levels; to the discovery of new knowledge through experimentation and research; to the publication of the results of investigation through scholarly and scientific journals and monographs; and to the extension of the service of the University to the State through its institutes, its library, its press, and its other facilities and faculties.

The four Presidents who guided the University through this period—Francis P. Venable, Edward Kidder Graham, Marvin H. Stacy, and Harry W. Chase—were closely tied through their commanding personalities and their unifying ideas. Certain members of the faculty who served with Venable before 1900 played important roles in the transition; this able group included William Dallam Toy, Henry Van Peters Wilson, Henry Horace Williams, M.C.S. Noble, Collier Cobb, C.S. Mangum, E.V. Howell, Archibald Henderson, T.J. Wilson, Jr., and G.M. McKie. These men were joined by a second group who became members of the staff between 1900 and 1910 and likewise contributed to the unity of objectives and ideas. They included Professors I.H. Manning, George Howe, N.W. Walker, W. deB. MacNider, W.C. Coker, J.G. deR. Hamilton, H.M. Wagstaff, W.M. Dey, P.H. Winston, A.S. Wheeler, R.B. Lawson, W.S. Bernard, J.M. Booker, G.K.G. Henry, J.G. Beard, T.F. Hickerson, Business Manager C.T. Woollen, and Librarian Louis R. Wilson.

In order to follow the transition from a good college of liberal arts to that of a modern university, it is necessary to have at least a partial picture of where and what the institution was when President E.A. Alderman resigned his distinguished Presidency in 1900 to go to the headship of Tulane University. The structural organization of the administration was simple. There was no dean of the College. Students who had occasion to consult with an officer went directly to the President, who in turn directed them to the appropriate professor or the registrar or bursar.

The students of 1900 had to find rooms in private homes or live in unfurnished dormitory rooms; arrange for meals either at Commons Hall ($8 per month board) or at eating places in the village at costs ranging from $6.50 to $13 per month; and move into college life without the benefit of an organized orientation program.

Joshua W. Gore, Professor of Physics, served as chairman of the curriculum committee and was the architect of the daily schedule of recitations. To the amazement and delight of his colleagues, he carried the

25. Louis Round Wilson, *The University of North Carolina, 1900-1930* (Chapel Hill: The University of North Carolina Press, 1957).

whole scheme of courses and hours of recitation in his head; he was a man who could resolve conflicts in much the manner of the skilled chess player who foresees the development of a dozen moves in advance.

The curricula of 1900 followed in direct descent from the early curriculum prepared by Samuel E. McCorkle, which emphasized somewhat English and the natural sciences; the modifications that had been made by President Caldwell and his associates from Princeton, who emphasized the classics and imported the latest scientific apparatus; the further changes due to the presence of the distinguished scientists, Denison Olmsted and Elisha Mitchell, from Yale, and President David L. Swain. Olmsted and Mitchell emphasized mathematics and the sciences, including agriculture. President Swain had stressed the importance of political economy, history and constitutional law. French, logic, and rhetoric had also found a place in the curriculum.

The School of Law had been established by William Horne Battle in 1845 as a private law school. The School was interrupted while the University was closed, and President Kemp P. Battle conducted it, in addition to his other duties, from 1879 to 1881 after his father's death. Judge John Manning relieved him in 1881 and continued as its head until his death in 1899; he was succeeded by Judge James C. MacRae.

The School of Medicine was established in 1879 by Thomas W. Harris, class of 1859, who had received his medical diploma from the University of New York and had then spent two years in hospital work at the famous École de Médecine in Paris. It was a private school, but its courses in the basic sciences were taught by the University. Dr. Harris resigned in 1885 and the School was discontinued until 1890, when Dr. Richard H. Whitehead, a graduate of the Medical School of the University of Virginia, became Professor of Anatomy, Physiology, and Materia Medica.

Dr. Harris was also the founder of the School of Pharmacy (1880), but it was not until 1898-1900 that the School experienced any major growth in enrollment. Howell, a graduate of the Philadelphia College of Pharmacy and former proprietor of a Rocky Mount drug store, taught 20 students in 1899.

The University Library, located in Smith Hall (Playmakers Theatre), contained 32,000 volumes and 12,000 pamphlets in 1900. The student body numbered 512, of which 93% were from North Carolina. Times were hard, and every means possible was utilized to get funds. Students competed for positions as waiters, dishwashers, printing office assistants, downtown shop clerks, and newspaper correspondents. There were few high schools in the state, and thus many students were not equipped to take college work in their stride. The academic mortality rate was high, and the percent of entering students to graduate four years later averaged 19.4% between the years 1875 and 1900.

The administration permitted the adoption of the honor system in 1875, and this first step in student self-government had been extended by 1900 to areas other than the conduct of quizzes and examinations.

The religious life of the University centered around the YMCA on the campus and the Sunday Schools and services of the churches of the village. Attendance at Chapel was compulsory for all students. W.F. Bryan was appointed the school's first cheerleader in 1899. Since there were no football seats or bleachers that year, the coaches' and officials' principal difficulty was to keep spectators off the playing field. It is noteworthy that Carolina won the 1898 showdown with Virginia because of the remarkable running of halfback Edward Vernon Howell—yes!—the head of the Pharmacy School.

Classrooms and living quarters were primitive in 1900. Rooms had simple drop electric lights, and heat came from coal stoves and open fireplaces. Such toilets, showers, and bathtubs as existed were located under the Library—entirely apart from all dormitories. When the 15-inch blizzard of 1899 struck, the whole campus holed up. One student, when asked when he was going to bathe, replied that he would do what he had done at home in the mountains: wait 'til spring.

. A youthful Francis P. Venable (left) enjoys a quiet moment beside a Chapel Hill pond.

Francis P. Venable—beloved chemistry professor, President, and a man who introduced an active UNC building program to the citizens of North Carolina.

Francis Preston Venable, President from 1900 to 1914, insisted upon sound, scholarly work; constantly maintained an objective, scientific point of view; and demonstrated unusual skill as a constructive organizer and builder. He admired, but lacked, the shrewd political-mindedness of President Winston in dealing with legislatures, and the warmth and perfection of Alderman as a platform speaker.

As a professor Venable, always the investigator, had developed the Bunsen burner in its present form. Not realizing the monetary value of his modification, Venable sold the right of its manufacture and sale for the sum of six burners. In 1893 Dr. Venable and William Rand Kenan, Jr. (UNC 1893) devised the chemical method for making calcium carbide in a furnace when owners of cotton mills at Spray, North Carolina, asked him to aid in the fight against a waste product which hindered some of their processes. He and Kenan developed a process for utilizing the waste product, calcium carbide, in making acetylene gas, but he received no financial benefit from the patent which covered the process. To Venable, his most important work was the training of expert chemists and imparting to them his zeal for scientific investigation.

Venable had a vision of a University "built and furnished such that every deserving and desiring son of the State and many from other states might find here the best and highest training that they need. I have come to the opinion," he said, "that luxury of equipment may sap the vitality of an institution as it does that of a man, and I greatly deprecate the increased scale of expenditure which must come with luxurious surroundings.

The Women's University Club, 1907

Our function is to train these men so that they may be capable of the highest possible service to God and country. The University's duty then lies clear before it without any possibility of mistaking."

Nationally and internationally the world, though moving towards World War I, was at peace when Venable's administration began. It fell between the Spanish-American and Boer Wars (1898-1900) and World War I (1914). It was a period, consequently, in which, without outside diversion, Venable could concentrate upon the problems of the University without having his attention diverted elsewhere. It was also a period from which the extreme poverty of the Battle administration had slowly receded, and in which North Carolina was painfully but surely building up economic resources with which public education could be supported.

With few exceptions the buildings of 1900 had been erected before the Civil War. To secure a new, adequate plant, Venable looked to four sources: the State; alumni and friends; philanthropic foundations and individuals; and the conversion of bequests and endowment into income-producing buildings and utilities. From these combined sources, and through purchase, he added sixteen buildings, bringing the total number on the campus in 1914 to twenty-eight; and, of even greater importance, he firmly established the assumption by the State of the responsibility of providing the major part of the University's physical plant, a plant which in June 1914, was valued at $1,008,400.

Venable directed much of his energy to strengthening the faculty. Because only 18% of the entering class in 1901 was graduated, Venable sought an enlarged faculty, resulting in smaller teacher/student ratios. He also emphasized the desirability of scholarships for the aid of needy students so that they would not have to spend as many hours working outside the classroom in order to pay their school expenses.

The Normal School of 1877-84 was the progenitor of the School of Education, which Venable placed firmly in the administration and academic structure of the University in 1913. It led first to the establishment of the Department of Pedagogy (later Education) under Professor Nelson B. Henry in 1885, and ultimately became the School of Education (1913) with Professor M.C.S. Noble as Dean.

During Venable's presidency the Library collection grew from 38,593 to 72,295 volumes; the total annual Library expenditures from $2,600 to $10,789; and the Library staff from three members to nine members.

The presidency of Edward Kidder Graham, including the year in which he served as Acting President, was short and crowded with achievement. It was compressed into five years, 1913-18, and was packed with his stimulating ideas, charged with his spirit of bold educational and civic adventure, and moved by his challenging, dynamic leadership.

Graham boldly extended the services of the University to the boundaries of the State; initiated the study of rural education, rural social economics, the dramatic arts, and business administration; built a strong faculty through the addition of distinguished scholars; skillfully won increased funds for maintenance and buildings; projected a systematic plan for campus development; advocated a sound student government and clean athletics; and, as Director for the South Atlantic States of the Students' Army Training Corps, gave his life in the service of his country.

As a student Graham had been a brilliant debater; and, with his classmate, W.J. Brogden, he won the 1898 debate with rival Georgia. Among other accomplishments, he was a charter member of the Order of the Gorgon's Head, and in 1897-98 he served as editor-in-chief of the *Tar Heel.*

Students, faculty members and the general public were in awe of the creative, contagious spirit of this man. Deeply spiritual in nature, Graham was a member of the Chapel Hill Presbyterian church, and he shared in its concern for the religious development of students through the churches of the community and the YMCA. In his Chapel talks he frequently dealt with the moral and religious problems of college life.

On May 8, 1917, just four weeks after war was declared with Germany, 125 students left the University for the officers' training camp at Oglethorpe, Georgia. Those among them who were seniors were awarded their degrees, provided their class work had been satisfactory up to May 1. At President Graham's urging hundreds of alumni joined the remaining faculty and students in overflowing Memorial Hall on June 6 for a patriotic Commencement at which Secretary of War Newton D. Baker and Secretary of the Navy Josephus Daniels (a UNC alumnus and later editor of the *Raleigh News and Observer*) were the principal speakers. By that date 250 UNC students and alumni were stationed at Camp Oglethorpe, and by the time school reopened in September, 500 students and faculty members were organized in four companies, and they drilled twelve hours a week under

The Pickwick Theatre, that infamous Franklin Street haunt, ran this ad in the 1913 Yack.

Edward Kidder Graham—UNC graduate, professor and President. He may well have had a positive influence on more lives in a shorter span of time than any other President in the school's history.

Franklin Street has been the site of a thousand parades—this one urging us to support "our boys" in World War I.

Four faculty members who joined the World War I effort: (left to right) Andrew Patterson, Charles Mangum, Felix Hickerson and James Bullitt.

Note the uniformed students standing tall before President Edward Kidder Graham at commencement ceremonies, 1917.

No coeds in blue jeans at this graduation (circa 1918).

Captain J. Stuart Allen. In an address to these men, Graham emphasized that "The issue of freedom is the *only* issue in this immediate and terrible task of those who 'would be free or die.'"

As a part of Graham's plan for training the University's men for war, football was eliminated, and many of those who had played it the previous autumn began receiving their daily exercise in a system of six-foot-deep trenches which were dug at the edge of Battle Park. Mr. Julius Cone of Greensboro presented the battalion with 250 outmoded Civil War rifles for drilling since modern rifles were not available. By May, 1918, the number of Carolina men in service rose to 1,185, and in August of that year the War Department converted the University into a unit of the Students' Army Training Corps.

In total the University contributed 2,240 of her students, alumni, and faculty to the war effort; 34 of them were killed in battle or lost their lives from other causes. President Graham spoke to his colleagues about his desire to enlist as a private, but a personal letter from President Woodrow Wilson, delivered by Secretary Daniels dissuaded him: "As your commander in chief I order you back to your post!" The President's letter convinced Graham that as head of the school he could direct many, but as a soldier he would count only as one.

But war was not the only tragedy of 1918. During the fall the most devastating flu epidemic in the state's history struck; more than 500 cases in October caused the infirmary and dormitories to overflow with flu patients. Victims of the devastating epidemic included three students, two nurses, and, just three weeks before the end of the war, President Edward Kidder Graham.

A man of great vision, Graham left behind the following challenge to Stacy, Chase, his cousin Frank, and others who would someday assume the President's chair: "The time has come when we should abandon the planless methods heretofore followed of waiting upon events, of attempting to solve each little problem as it arises, and of managing the affairs of the University day by day with no thought of what the future may bring forth. We ought to be forward-looking, to study the University in terms of the needs of the State, to formulate a large and definite plan for its future development so that we may have a certain, well-defined end to which to work, and in all our work adhere strictly to that plan. We ought to have for our own guidance well-thought-out plans of the Greater Statewide University, of fifty, even a hundred years hence, with the whole State for its campus and every citizen of the State for a member of its student body, and we ought to familiarize the people of the State with our plans, our hopes and our ambitions."

On October 31, 1918, the Trustees appointed to the presidency Marvin H. Stacy, a fine Christian teacher and administrator who had served as Dean of the College of Liberal Arts under Graham. The influenza epidemic which had struck down his predecessor would claim Stacy as a victim just 83 days later. During that brief tenure Stacy made several important contributions to the University's future. Most notable were his recommendations, later accepted, that a school of commerce be established; a music director be hired; the Law School be expanded; a "woman's building" be created; and a health officer and publications editor be appointed.

Though still mired in the shock and sorrow caused by the loss of many sons to a world war and two presidents to influenza, the University family clearly made a brilliant choice by electing Harry Woodburn Chase its tenth president. Serving from 1919 to 1930, Chase would later be called "the Architect of the Modern University," and for good reason. During his eleven years as president the following buildings and facilities were added to the University's campus: Phillips Hall, Steele, Archer House (purchased), Grimes, Manly, Ruffin, Mangum, Saunders, Murphey, Manning (Law), the "Tin Can," Aycock, Graham, Lewis, the Carolina Inn (gift from the Hill family), Spencer, Venable, Greenhouse, Kenan Stadium (gift from the Kenan family), Everett, Bingham, the Library, Graham Memorial, and the Morehead-Patterson Bell Tower (gift from those two families).

President Chase possessed an ability to think in terms of ideas and principles rather than in concrete situations and personalities. Never was this quality more clearly displayed than during the controversy over the Poole bill, a 1925 legislative measure which would have outlawed the teaching of evolution in State-supported institutions. Chase knew that the proposed bill violated the basic academic principle upon which the concept of a university was based, i.e., the freedom to teach, investigate and publish.

Beloved and respected by faculty and students alike, Marvin H. Stacy served as UNC's President for only a matter of weeks before succumbing to the tragic flu epidemic of 1918–19.

Specifically, the publication in the *Journal of Social Forces* of two articles which, when taken out of context, particularly offended a number of churchmen in the State, and the selection of several McNair lecturers who were not philosophically aligned with Reverend W.P. McCorkle, led to a bill which read: "...It is the sense of the General Assembly... of North Carolina that it is injurious to the welfare of the people... for any official or teacher in the State, paid wholly or in part by taxation, to teach or permit to be taught as a fact either Darwinism or any other evolutionary hypothesis that links man in blood relationship with any lower form of life." This resolution had been introduced in the House of Representatives by D. Scott Poole of Hoke County, and he was vigorously supported by the Reverend J.R. Pentuff, a Baptist minister from Concord.

In opposing the resolution before the Committee on Education and later in the *Tar Heel,* Chase said: "I am not here to discuss evolution as a biologist, but to speak in behalf of human liberty... The constitution of the United States guarantees freedom of speech and freedom of the press; it declares that those freedoms shall not be abridged. Shall we write into that article 'except to school teachers'?"

That same week Chase wrote Representative Walter Murphy, UNC class of 1892: "If the Poole bill should pass, the University will find it impossible to retain the services of many of its best men, who feel that their self respect will be impaired should they have to work under such restrictions. If anybody is interested in dismantling the University, no surer way could be found in my judgment."

Chase rallied the University's forces and the bill was defeated, but it was by no means a dead issue. A year later a "Committee of 100" was organized in Charlotte, where some 300 fundamentalist ministers and laymen gathered to plan a new bill which would require the dismissal of teachers not meeting the requirement of the legislation. In a heated debate Greensboro School Board member E.D. Broadhurst (UNC 1899) squared off with Methodist minister J. Walter West of Lincolnton, with Broadhurst emphatically declaring: "The Bible does not need any help from the North Carolina Legislature."

Two months later a Superior Court Judge in Shelby was quoted as follows: "It has been said that 40 percent of the boys sent out from the University are atheists or agnostics. The atmosphere is there, and the President and the instructors make it." That statement was challenged in the press by Professors R.D.W. Connor and J.F. Royster of the University faculty.

Then, in 1927, Poole introduced a second bill molded from his first famous proposal. A vigorous debate ensued, and, dramatically, it was a UNC law student—Paul J. Ranson (1922)—who helped convince lawmakers to defeat the bill through his stirring oration: "I was raised in a Christian home, I have attended the University for six years counting law school, and I haven't been driven out of the church yet! I've had five brothers who went to the University, and not one of them has turned out an atheist. I don't know what made me get up here... I just couldn't sit back there and listen to all this foolishness." Following a round of applause, the bill was soon voted down by a 25 to 11 margin.

Chase's leadership during the Poole bill controversy was the crowning glory of his administration and a decisive demonstration of the full-grown stature and maturity of the University.

A final characteristic that differentiated Chase from the administrators of other Southern institutions of higher education was his insistence upon the attainment and maintenance of national standards. For him, to attain "the best in the South" fell far short of the mark. Chase strove for high achievement on a national scale in the new fields developed during his presidency: commerce, drama, music, psychology, sociology, research in social sciences, publication, the enhancement of the library, and support of graduate work. Emphasis on these objectives led to the University's admission into the Association of American Universities in 1922—and to the high regard in which he and the University came to be held by other American institutions.

Harry W. Chase was one of the University's ablest Presidents—and a staunch defender of the cause of freedom of speech when that freedom seemed in jeopardy.

U.S. President William Howard Taft (center) with Judge Henry G. Connor (left) and President Edward Kidder Graham.

This photo captured Dr. Richard Whitehead's Medical School class during a lesson in bedside manners.

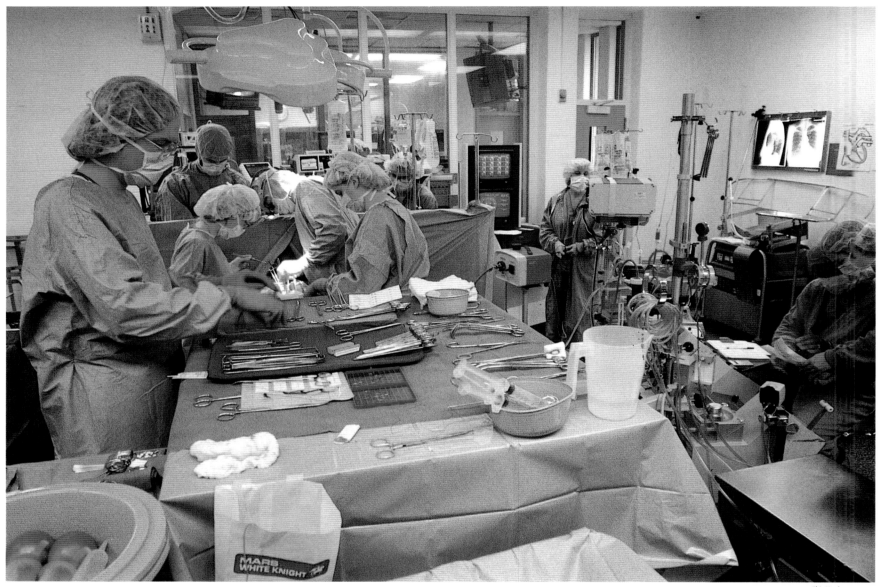

Open heart surgery, a procedure still awesome to much of the public, has been performed at North Carolina Memorial Hospital for 30 years. The cardiac surgery group, headed by Professor Benson Wilcox, performed the hospital's first heart transplants in 1986.

An open heart surgery team at NCMH works skillfully to repair a damaged valve in a patient's heart.

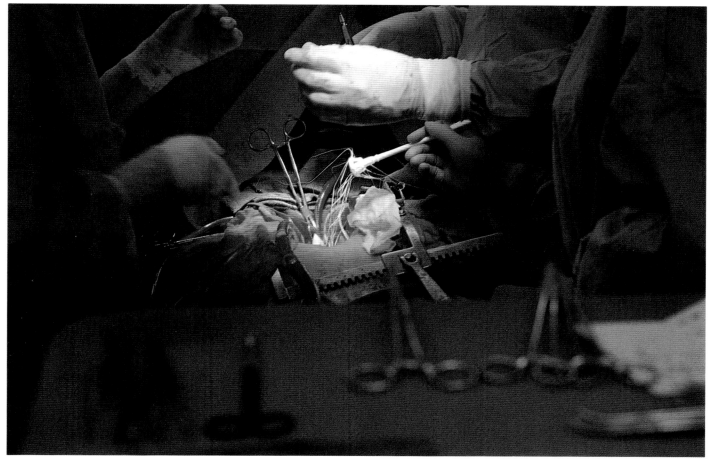

An aerial view of the University campus in 1919 includes Franklin Street and the automobiles of the privileged few.

THE VILLAGE, 1924

by Hazel Trimble

My husband and I moved to Chapel Hill in 1924. We lived in a cottage behind Mrs. Bain's boarding house. The village was much different then, of course; in fact, there were only two or three automobiles in town, and no paved streets except for a narrow paved strip along Franklin Street. The sidewalks were of gravel, which is part of the reason why I remember Chapel Hill of 1924 as being very, *very* muddy.

A man named Pendergraft ran a bus between Chapel Hill and Durham, or any place you wanted to go, and that was the only way to get to Durham in those days. As cars became fashionable people began making trips over there, always asking their friends in advance if they could "pick up anything for you." There was a bakery in Durham that always had delicious rolls, so frequently we would order a batch when friends were going that way.

At that time there were only three main stores in the village, including the one that later became Fowler's. Believe it or not, they would cut up your fresh meat for you right out in the street in front of the store. And it wasn't just a food store: they carried bolts of material, threads and needles, too. There was only one drug store—Eubanks'—and it served as the "loafing place" for all the men in town. They had a bench right inside the front door; that's where the men sat and gossiped and watched the women go by. Back then you'd call up your friends and say, "Meet me at Eubanks' and we'll have a Coca-Cola." They had fountain drinks in those days.

Chapel Hill was certainly a more sociable town then. If you were driving up the street and saw somebody you knew, you'd both stop your cars and have a conversation right in the middle of Franklin Street. Whenever a new faculty member came to town, there was always a big tea; everyone was invited. There was more "general entertaining" for everyone back then, rather than the parties for special, smaller groups like we have today. President and Mrs. Chase held an open house every Thursday night for anyone who wanted to join them for tea.

As delightful as Chapel Hill was, though, I still can't understand how it got so muddy. Boys had to roll their trousers up to their knees to keep the mud off. And as for your shoes, well, everywhere you went you had to wear shoes for which you had no respect.

UNC HISTORY, 1900-1986,

As reported in the Yackety Yacks

With grateful thanks to Louis Round Wilson, William Friday, Karen Parker, Tom Wicker and some 40 other authors who have chronicled much of the school's history in the essays found elsewhere in this volume, the editors turn now to the past 86 years of Carolina life as preserved in that most remarkable of volumes, the *Yack*. Imagine the fun we had researching those works—glimpsing at, reading about, and in a certain sense reliving the student years of Thomas Wolfe and Frank Porter Graham, Luther Hodges and James Worthy, Robyn Hadley and Sue Walsh! Stored safely in the North Carolina Collection on the fifth floor of Wilson Library, the *Yacks* hold great adventure and many smiles for all students and alumni. Treat yourself to an hour or two in the North Carolina Collection sometime. You will be astonished at how similar the students of 1987 are to the students of 1901. Fortunately for all, you'll see clearly just how far we have come as a people in that brief span of time.

A word of apology: Some 130,000 of us will not find our names in these next few pages. Matter of fact, you may not find the name of your dorm(s), fraternity, sorority, or favorite professor either. You may even have been an All-American at something and not be officially remembered herein, and for that we are sorry. Carolina is a *big* school. But if you will approach these pages with an open mind and a happy heart, you'll find just as much joy as we did. Even though most of us didn't make Phi Beta Kappa, the varsity basketball team or head cheerleader, we too were young, unencumbered by our parents' job deadlines, carpools, ulcers, and house payments. We had fun, didn't we? So enjoy!

John Sprunt Hill   NC Collection

1901 Volume One. Published "by the fraternities and literary societies of the University. . . and dedicated to John Sprunt Hill, whose brilliant professional career and true loyalty to his alma mater prove him an alumnus worthy of our esteem."

Listed were all 36 members of the faculty. There were 150 freshmen on campus in the fall of 1897, and only 52 of them stayed long enough to graduate in 1901.

Each class had a yell. For example, the class of 1902 vigorously roared, "Rah, rah, rah—zip, rah, zoo—razoo, razoo—Nineteen Two !!" Not to be outdone, those two years behind rebounded with a resounding, "Rip! Rah! Rah!—Rip! Rah! Roar!—We are the class of 1904 !!" Coeds were treated somewhat differently in 1901; in fact, all 13 of them were pictured on the same page —not far from a 38-line poem entitled "Ye Coy Coed."

The student body got every bit as wound up over the annual debates with the University of Georgia as future students would over basketball games with Dook and State. Arguing such subjects as the potential annexation of Hawaii, UNC edged the Bulldogs in 1901. . . and later in '04, '05, '07 and '08.

The *Tar Heel* was published every Monday as "the official organ of the University Athletic Association." Football scores included a 55-0 win over Georgia; 48-0 over Vanderbilt; and 38-0 over (Huh?) D.D.I. of Morganton. Ads in the back of the *Yack* included one from Pickard's Livery Feed and Sale Stables: "Horses, buggies, and carriages to let at all hours. Rates low." The Medical College of Virginia ran a recruitment ad.

1902 The Guitar and Mandolin Club boasted a membership of 16; the Chapel Choir had ten members; the Wilmington Club 12 members; and the Mecklenburg Club 38 members (including Edward Kidder Graham). The football team played two games against North Carolina Agricultural and Mechanical College of Raleigh (name was shortened later to Moo U), winning both (39-0, 30-0). The Law School and the Med School each had a football team, but the varsity wouldn't play them.

The Idiotic Order of Goos had a full page: Calvin Blackwell of Wilmington won the All-Around Goo Award; he was also voted "Chief Bearer of the Brainless Cranium" on Washington's Birthday. Ernest Leggett of Palmyra was selected "Dog-faced Man;" Joe Speight of Wrendale was "Missing Link."

1903 The faculty numbered 64, the student body 608. There were ten scientific laboratories, the library had 40,000 volumes, *and* the school proudly advertised that it had installed *electric* lights. The *Yack* dedicated a full page to the school's three coeds: Ellen John Faison, Anna McQueen, and Nellie Roberson. Charles T. Woollen edited the yearbook; Nathan W. Walker edited the *Tar Heel;* and Charles

Phillips Russell was editor of the *University Magazine.*

NC Collection

Distinguished student, author and professor: Charles Phillips Russell.

The Dialectic Society (formerly the Debating Society) boasted 147 members; the Philanthropic Literary Society had 107 members; and the South Carolina Club had 17 members. Daniel, Allen & Company of Raleigh carried an ad stating that they sold "leather shoes worth $5.00 for only $3.50."

1904 Both the Dialectic and Philanthropic societies had more members than in 1903. The varsity tennis team had two members; the Second Year Medical baseball team had 13 players; and the Faculty Butterfly Club had six members.

1905 The University had six coeds, two of whom were married. Football players' weights were listed, and two of the starters tipped the scales at 146 pounds. The Buncombe County Club had 24 members; the Pug Dog Club had ten members; and there were 14 men in the Nursery Club.

1906 The *Yack* was dedicated to Kemp Plummer Battle, LL.D., "who, as President, successfully rescued the University from ruin and decay, and brought it back to life of a wider usefulness and deeper scholarship than it had ever known before."

This *Yack* carried an essay by coed Mary Graves, who reported: "So far the coed has had no part in college life. She has been an outsider." The Florida Club had eight members; there were nine in the Hot Air Club. The various members of the Curleyhead Club were divided as follows: "Curls—14"; "Kinks—4"; "Shockheads—2"; "Topknots—5"; and "Roaches—2." Four companies carried ads for shotguns; one company advertised coffins.

The Central Hotel on Franklin Street, circa 1898.

1907 Miss Daisy Allen managed the senior class football team, which lost games to both the sophomore and junior classes. The Oak Ridge Club had 28 members.

1908 The reader should note that student life oft portends greater things in the wide beyond. Junior class debater Frank Porter Graham and his partner R.A. Freeman won the heated Sophomore-Junior Debate. The subject: "Should U.S. Senators be elected by a direct vote of the people?" (Ed. note: For more about U.S. Senator Frank P. Graham, see Tom Wicker's essay.)

Both members of the tennis team apparently wore neckties during their matches. The Cuban Club had seven members; the Buies Creek Club had 21 members; and the Bald-Head Club had 18 members. Jefferson Standard Life Insurance Company advertised that "insuring your life" with them "is the perfect consummation of patriotism and sound business judgment." Pickard's Hotel ad: "Hot and cold baths; an electric bell in every room." Fat's Barber Shop ad claimed they had a cure for dandruff, and Gowan's Pneumonia Cure ran an ad bearing the endorsement of Governor R.B. Glenn.

1909 Frank "Laddie Buck" Graham, at 125 pounds, was president of a senior class that included Kemp D. Battle, Frank P. Borden, Oscar Coffin, James Gordon Hanes, Francis Edward Winslow, and Norman Stockton.

A new sport emerged on campus that year, and Frank Graham was a member of that historic first team. There is no record that any games were played that year. It was called "basket ball."

The Weak-kneed Club had 14 members; the Spoony-Moony Bunch also had 14 members; and the Giraffe Club, 9 members. The Durham Automobile Company advertised their availability for "picnic parties and moonlight rides." The town of Wrightsville Beach promoted its proximity to nearby Wilmington: "Only 30 minutes by electric trains."

Oscar "Skipper" Coffin, distinguished Professor of Journalism for 30 years.

1910 Miss Helen Wharton of Waynesville was given a full page in the *Yack* and designated "President, Vice President and Treasurer of the Coeds."

1911 The senior class voted Jim Cheshire of Raleigh "Best Egg." Independent Dental Parlors of Durham (phone number 630) advertised "Gold fillings for $1.00 up, silver fillings 50¢ up, extractions 25¢ up."

1912 Perhaps Elon College should've gone into the Four Corners: They lost to the UNC basketballers by a 36 to 5 score. The Durham YMCA beat Carolina in a thriller, 29 to 28. Franklin Chewing Gum advertised that "Athletes and others everywhere chew Franklin Gum because it aids digestion, whitens the teeth and purifies the breath."

1913 Senior class superlatives: Jim Carter, "Biggest Bluffer"; John Workman, "Biggest Tightwad"; Brush Wilson, "Biggest Loafer." The basketball team beat Davidson by a 42 to 8 margin. There were 153 members of the Dialectic Literary Society; the Philanthropic Literary Society had 202 members. Student leader: Kenneth C. Royall.

1914 The following description of exams was given: "Exams. . . an unrestful time of tension, of anxiety. . . a tendays' bad dream. . . an awful time. Much more of it and we feel that life would really not be worth the weary struggle. At length even this period of horror expires. . . notebooks are lost, and textbooks begin to accumulate the accustomed dignity of dust."

1915 Austin Carr, "Biggest Social Bug"; Bob Fitzgerald, "Biggest Bluffer"; B.F. Paty, "Best Egg." Football score: UNC 65, Virginia Medical College 0. Winner of the Colonial Dames History Prize: would-be Senator Samuel J. Ervin, Jr. Junior Class Historian and debate winner: would-be Governor William B. Umstead. Robert B. House was elected vice president of the senior class. Enrollment had risen to 1,123; the faculty increased to 98.

1916 Junior Class Historian Sam Ervin Jr., wrote: "We have instituted a plan of holding 'smokers' monthly in order that the members of the class might be drawn into more binding ties of friendship." Graduates included Robert H.W. Welch, the man who would soon be founding father of the John Birch Society.

1917 Senior Class Historian Ervin wrote: "It might be well to state that hazing vanished completely the year *before* our class arrived, and that we have done much to keep this relic of barbarism in its grave." He was voted "Most Popular" and "Best Egg."

1918 Albert M. Coates, who would later create the UNC Institute of Government, won the North Carolina Intercollegiate Peace Oratorical Contest; he was also chosen president of the junior class.

Tall Thomas Wolfe of Asheville and his happy friend E.A. Griffin of Goldsboro, 1918.

1919 A sad school year: In a four-month period Presidents Graham, Stacy and Battle died, with only the latter dying after reaching his retirement years. Editor of the *Tar Heel,* Assistant Editor of the *Magazine,* and a Playmakers and Satyrs leader: Thomas Clayton Wolfe of Asheville. He would later write *Look Homeward Angel, Of Time and the River, The Web and the Rock,* and *You Can't Go Home Again.* President of the senior class was Luther H. "Luke" Hodges, a student who "imbued the entire campus with his spirit." The *Yack* editor wrote: "Luke will make good," prophetic words describing a future Governor and U.S. Secretary of Commerce.

1920 Rising leader: William Donald Carmichael, Jr. Jonathan Worth Daniels began a career in newspapering at the twice-weekly *Tar Heel.*

1921 Carmichael: Managing Editor of the *Tar Heel.* Adeline E. Hughes: "Prettiest Coed."

1922 Daniels edited the *Tar Heel.* George Watts Hill was Assistant Editor of the *Yack.* The fine UNC Press was founded this year.

1923 Thomas Turner: "Best Egg." Sam Cathey: "Biggest Politician." Roy Morris: "Ugliest." And you thought only Dook students would make such remarks?

1924 Forty new tennis courts were built, along with two athletic fields—one for a sport called "Pushball." The Wolfpack lost a heartbreaker to Carolina's basketball squad, 44 to 9. During the fall the school staged its first cake race. One hundred cakes were donated by the ladies of Chapel Hill, and following a big, free-for-all cross-country race, the winners and everyone else in the village ate you-know-what. Later that year hundreds of students joined in a tug-o-war in front of the Old Well.

1925 Arnold K. King was tapped as "Prophet" of his class and into Phi Beta Kappa membership. And as for fearless *Yack* predictions: "We hereby prophesy for 'Red' Jonas a brilliant success in the legal world." The editors felt that if North Carolina would ever elect a Republican to anything, Jonas would be the man: "He is President of the Dialectic Senate. . . an intercollegiate debater, and the recognized leader of a small but faithful bank of Republicans." Charles R. Jonas would later serve umpteen terms in Congress.

1926 The first year coeds were displayed in the *Yack* as beauty queens.

1927 Kay Kyser: Carolina Playmakers; Wig and Masque; Producer of "That Y Minstrel;" Di Minstrel Revue; Black and

Charles R. Jonas, "Mr. Republican" NC Collection

White Revue; Chief Cheerleader. A year later he was leader of a nine-man orchestra. Dan K. Moore graduated; in 1964 he would become the 31st UNC grad to be elected Governor of North Carolina.

Sophomore Walter Spearman was Assistant Editor of both the *Yack* and the *Tar Heel* and a member of the editorial board of the *Buccaneer.* Ceasar Cone was Business Manager of the *Yack;* his counterpart at the Buccaneer was Holt McPherson.

NC Collection
Football hero Charlie "Choo Choo" Justice (left) and entertainer/musician/band leader Kay "The Old Professor" Kyser, a grad of the Kollege of Musical Knowledge.

1928 Give credit to Vic Huggins, head cheerleader, for establishing Rameses as the school's mascot. Edward A. Cameron was Senior Class Prophet. Associate Editor of the *Carolina Magazine:* Shepperd Strudwick. Baseball team goes 16-2 to win "State Championship."

1929 Nine-story Wilson Library, which could house 400,000 books, was completed at a cost of $625,000. Walter Spearman was voted "Most Brilliant," "Most Influential," President of Phi Beta Kappa, and President of the North Carolina Collegiate Press Association. Bowman Gray, Jr. managed the track team and was President of the German Club.

Suzie Marshall Sharp made Law Review for the second time, was Secretary/Treasurer of her third-year Law class. She would later be the first woman to hold the office of Chief Justice of the North Carolina Supreme Court.

The track team won the state championship for the seventh straight year. Camel cigarettes carried a full-page *color* ad.

Suzie Sharp made Law Review twice in the late 1920's, and later she honored her profession as the first woman Chief Justice of the North Carolina Supreme Court.

1930 George Bernard Shaw wrote the *Yack* dedication to Drama Professor Archibald Henderson. Gordon Gray was Phi Beta Kappa and manager of the baseball team.

1931 Newly-elected President of the consolidated University, Dr. Frank Porter Graham, expressed the University's gratitude for the students' willingness to accept less in the way of services during the financial crisis caused by the Depression: "In this year, distinctive for the. . . Depression and an unconquerable spirit, you have mightily helped the University to come through. You have borne the deep budget cut in a spirit that rises above its damaging gashes and that will hold on for the better day that is to come."

The three institutions comprising the consolidated University were UNC, North Carolina College for Women (now UNC-G), and North Carolina State College of Agriculture and Engineering in Raleigh. The *Tar Heel* became the first college daily in the South. Beverly Moore and Joe Colin Eagles were officers of Phi Beta Kappa, and Eagles was voted "Best Student."

1932 The Depression had not ended, nor had the student body's uncompromising love for the University. President Graham wrote these words of thanks: "In this most critical year in the life of the University in the present century, the student body has stood like a rock in a storm. With hundreds of students faced with the necessity of going back to bankrupt homes and jobless towns, the student body started off the Emergency Loan Fund with $2,000. With a budget cut to a destructive point, they put into the budget a saving spiritual power. The student body of 1931-32 will always be memorable for this contribution to the high tradition of this place. May their faith and courage carry over into the making of a nobler commonwealth. Wherever they may go, Alma Mater will always reach across the continent and across the years and hold them tight to her great heart."

Hamilton Hobgood: President of the Senior Class; Order of the Golden Fleece; "Biggest Politician." Billy Arthur: Head Cheerleader.

1933
The University's budget was 54% lower than it had been in 1929. The tennis team won its forty-eighth straight match.

1934
Tennis team: National Champs, so *they* said. James M. Tatum was singled out as a great punt blocker in football, but UNC was still drubbed by Georgia and Duke, 30-0 and 21-0. Carl Snavely took over from Coach C.C. Collins, and thanks to players like Tatum and George Barclay, gridiron fortunes changed overnight.

Hugh Morton

In 1934 George Barclay was called "the most nationally-known Carolina student of all time."

1935
It was a very good year: The Depression was behind them; appropriations were partially restored; the *Yack* was voted an All-American publication by the National Scholastic Press; Coach Bob Fetzer's track team won its thirteenth consecutive state championship; the basketball team (called the White Phantoms, not the Tar Heels) went 23-2; and George Barclay, called "the most nationally-known Carolina student of all time," led the football team to a 7-1-1 record. Bad news for the tennis team, though: After 74 consecutive victories—an intercollegiate record—the netters bowed to Princeton. Graduates included Vermont Royster, would-be editor of the *Wall Street Journal.*

NC Collection

Vermont Connecticut Royster, class of 1935, served for many years as editor of The Wall Street Journal. *A Pulitzer Prize winner, Royster displayed keen wisdom by forsaking New York for the good life of professorship in Chapel Hill.*

1936
In football Carolina beat Wake Forest, Maryland, Davidson, Georgia Tech, VMI and Virginia by a combined score of 197 to 0!! Basketball: 21 wins, four losses. Tennis: 18 wins, one loss. Track: Fourteenth consecutive state championship.

1937
Football: Eight wins, two losses. Tennis: Undefeated; took its record to 108 wins, two losses since 1929.

1938
Student Legislature founded. Carolina Inn became "an inn, faculty social center and alumni headquarters." On December 5th President Graham presented an Honorary Doctorate of Laws to President Franklin D. Roosevelt.

1939
The first May Court sported 14 beauty queens. Woollen Gym was completed. Swimming became an official sport. Tennis: 10-2-1.

1940
Another great year. The Institute of Government moved into its own building; Navy ROTC was established; and the *fencing* team won its third consecutive Southern Championship. Swimming: 7-1; tennis: 19-0, with the "streak" since 1929 raised to 171-4. Basketball: Junior All-America George "Blind Bomber" Glamack led Coach Bill Lange's squad to the Southern Conference title. Track: Undefeated indoors and outdoors. . . considered the school's greatest track team ever. Football: 8-1-1.

President of the Student Body: James Evans Davis (later a brilliant physician). And consider these other well-known Tar Heel leaders who were picked by their peers to manage student government and the publications: Edward L. Rankin, Jr., George Watts Carr, Jr., Hargrove "Skipper"Bowles, Ike Grainger, William Dees and Bill Snider.

1941
Coeds were added to the cheerleading squad for the first time, and card displays were used at several football games. "Yackety Yack," a cheer/yell originated by Kay Kyser, was revived; it became a great favorite with Kenan Stadium crowds. And look who led student government and publications in 1941: Terry Sanford, Skipper Bowles (fourth straight year on Honor Council), Alabaman Truman Hobbs (who defeated Ferebee Taylor for Student Body President), Hugh Morton (Chapel Hill's Ansel Adams), Bill "Scoop" Snider, Orville "Double Scoop" Campbell, and Louis Harris (who would become a world-famous pollster).

Publisher Orville Campbell

1942
On December 7, 1941, the Japanese attacked Pearl Harbor and Chapel Hill became a changed community overnight. (Ed. note: See Orville Campbell's essay). Within a week the Carolina Volunteer Training Corps, the brainchild of sophomore Henry Wisebram, sprang up spontaneously, giving students the opportunity to learn the fundamentals of military drill. An office of Student Civilian Defense was established—complete with trial black-outs. Students in upper quadrangle dorms found themselves giving up their rooms at the close of the winter quarter so that Navy personnel could move in.

While not every student supported the war effort, the Yack editors reported that "student ingenuity appeared as boys attempting to get into V-7 and other branches of the service resorted to memorizing eye charts, taking stretching exercises, and undergoing all sorts of weight-losing and weight-gaining diets, in order to pass physical exam requirements (Ed. Note: For a look at UNC during Vietnam War days, see Eric Calhoun's essay).

"Hammered by the challenge of the times, boys changed to men, casting aside youthful frivolity, taking up with grim determination the burdens that only a man's stout mind can conquer. Where saddle shoes had lackadaisically shuffled along shady walks, the rhythmic beat of a military tread now raised the dust. We rose with the sun to meet eight o'clock classes, and it was a new sense of duty to nation and to self that pulled us from beneath warm blankets to hurry forth in the hush of a chill dawn."

1943 Despite World War II, there were still signs of normal living, exams and sports, although schedules and rosters were dramatically changed. There was still an Honor Council (headed by Bert Bennett) and a Comptroller (former Wall Street whiz, Billy Carmichael). Princeton *again* snapped UNC's long tennis win streak—this time after 66 consecutive victories.

The number of Navy men on campus grew to 1,875 in 1943, and said sailors occupied ten campus dorms. Under the leadership of Commanders O.O. "Scrappy" Kessing and John P. Graff, the Navy school was called "the greatest physical toughening program that our armed forces have ever attempted."

1944 Most of the senior photos of 1944 were of young men in uniforms. At every turn the student body and faculty had to adjust to changes. Suddenly, most of the basketball opponents were military teams: Camp Butner, 309th Bombers, Cherry Point, Fort Bragg, Fort Jackson, and Seymour Johnson Air Force Base. And would you believe that *Navy* beat UNC's otherwise undefeated tennis team!?

President Frank Porter Graham spent his weeks in Washington working for the War Labor Board; on weekends "he came home to Chapel Hill to set the University in order."

1945 May 8: V-E Day! The War in Europe ended! September 2: V-J Day! Japan signed a formal surrender in Tokyo Bay (on the USS *Missouri*)! The village community was ecstatic. It was a time to rejoice, regroup and rebuild. UNC in 1945 was a school of 66 buildings, 1,638 acres, and 5,000 students (including 1,000 coeds). Lt. G.L. Carnevale's White Phantom basketball team went 19 and 6. Carl Snavely returned to coach football. And the boys came home!

NC Collection

Jubilant students Margaret Woodhouse and Gene Johnstone review the happiest news of 1945: "Peace, Japs Quit"

1946 Fun times! Dancing, crowded classrooms, and liberated hearts! The basketball team was led by Horace "Bones" McKinney, and the track and swim teams were more or less led by Bynum Hunter and Willis Casey. What happened to the tennis team (3 wins, 6 losses)? Sadie Hawkins Day was revived!

1947 Hundreds of veterans descended on an already overcrowded University, causing administrators to erect a village of Quonset huts, trailers, and barracks— whatever was required to make room for the troopers-turned-students-again. The *Yack* was dedicated to the great Sugar Bowl football team, a squad well-hyped by *Tar Heel* sports editor Irwin Smallwood. The swim team won 27 straight! Basketball, track and tennis: each was almost undefeated.

1948 Choo, choo, choo: the footballers chugged to an eight and two season, including a 34-7 trouncing of mighty Texas (Ed. note: See Neale Patrick's essay). The Carolina Forum was founded to bring interesting speakers to campus. *Tarnation,* a student humor magazine, hit the newsstands. Vic Seixas led the undefeated tennis team. And coed Julia Taylor, seated on the grass under a flowering Carolina cherry tree, was a pretty picture indeed. Life was good again.

1949 It was rumored that a new gizmo called "television" was about to be experimented with by the radio folks in Swain Hall. The newest of the deans was William C. Friday, who graduated from that school in Raleigh. The Tommy Dorsey Orchestra played at Midwinters. "Cabin parties" were big. Dalton Ruffin won his first election: Freshman Class President. Footballers, led by All-Americans Charles Justice and Arthur Weiner, won nine, tied one, and almost whipped Oklahoma in the Sugar Bowl. Baseball: NCAA semi-finalists. Soccer and track: Southern Conference champions.

1950 Dr. Frank Graham was appointed to the U.S. Senate. Harvie Ward was the second UNC golfer to win the NCAA championship. Seixas, Justice, Weiner and Kenny Powell led great tennis and football teams (Ed. Note: See essays by Neale Patrick, A.J. Carr and Charlie Justice). Eleanor Roosevelt was a Carolina Forum speaker; Gene Krupa drummed up a lot of support for the Germans officers. "Card stunts" at football games were *the* hit of the year. In Yankee Stadium (versus Notre Dame) Carolina students held up cards depicting the skyline of New York, and then, to the delight of onlookers across the field, illuminated the paper buildings with yellow lights they twinkled in their laps. As breathtaking as that was, many observers said it couldn't hold a candle to the stunt displayed at the Virginia game: It was (no joke) *animated,* and pictured Justice passing a *moving* ball to Weiner, who (of course) caught it for a touchdown.

1951 Gordon Gray was the new President of UNC. Built at a cost of $3 million, Morehead Planetarium opened. So did the Dentistry School. Rolfe Neil was managing editor of the *Tar Heel;* Jake Froelich ran Germans; Cecil B. DeMille selected the May Queen and her court; and General Omar Bradley and Edward R. Murrow spoke to the student body.

1952 The *Tar Heel* and the *Yack* each had its first-ever woman editor (Glenn Abbott Harden and Sue Lindsey, respectively). Jimmy Kilgo was Communication Club President. Press Club was formed, as was the University Symphony Orchestra (50 students, faculty members and townspeople—three concerts). Golf: 15 and 1. Football (Ugh!): 2 and 8.

On October 3rd and 4th headlines told of a polio wave that shocked the school and the nation. Two football games were cancelled, but, gratefully, four of the five athletes at UNC who contracted the disease returned to school later that winter.

1953 Student leaders: Ham Horton (who would later make it big in politics), Louie Patseavouras (who would later make it big in plastic surgery), Joel Fleishman, and Frank Daniels, Jr. There was a new basketball coach in Woollen Gym: Frank McGuire.

1954 You have to see it to believe it: Six coeds are mud wrestling in this 1954 photo, and dozens of on-looking male students are *howling!* George Barclay was the new football coach, and a new conference—the ACC—came on the scene. John Kenfield's tennis team went 23 and 0! Lib Moore edited the *Yack.* Jimmy and Tommy Dorsey played at Spring Germans.

1955 Wilmington native Charles Kuralt edited the *Tar Heel;* Ed Yoder was his able assistant. Runner Jim Beatty—only a soph—set three track records. This seems to have been the first year UNC elected a Homecoming Queen. But the big news concerned a skinny New Yorker named Lennie Rosenbluth and his basketball teammates. Said the *Yack,* "Because of Coach McGuire. . . people are looking to the near future when he will be able to remove the Wolfpack's basketball domination."

1956 Luther Hodges, Jr. (sporting a nice crew-cut) was Consolidated University Student Council President. John Young managed WUNC radio. Lennie and the roundballers went 17 and 4. Les Brown's Band played at Midwinters. Track and tennis: ACC champs.

1957 William Friday was elected Consolidated University President. Jim Tatum was football coach. Swim team brought their 17-year record to 130-17. James G. Exum, Jr., who would later be elected Chief Justice of the North Carolina Supreme Court, was Phi Beta

Kappa President and Honor Council Chairman. Hodges was Student Council Chairman, crew-cut notwithstanding. And another flat-topped Tar Heel, Joe Quigg, left the basketball world breathless for a few seconds when he casually canned two last-minute free throws to help the 'Heels notch the NCAA basketball championship (Ed. note: See essay by Bob Timberlake). It was a *very* good year.

Jim Exum, President of Phi Beta Kappa and Honor Council Chairman at UNC, later became Chief Justice of the North Carolina Supreme Court.

1958 Student leaders included Kelly Maness (Student Council Chairman), George Ragsdale, and Charles Graham. *Ram and Ewe,* a student humor publication, came and went quickly at 35¢ per copy. After eight losing seasons, the footballers go 6 and 4.

1959 Cameron Cooke did a *splendid* job as *Yack* editor; Bob Foxworth brought new spirit to the art of cheerleading; York Larese's free throw shooting style was copied by every kid in the state; Wade Smith was Junior Class President; and Dean E. Smith was an assistant basketball coach. UNC, now integrated, had two Black students on the YMCA board. Good Guys 50, Bad Guys 0 in the annual football battle with Dook! Law School graduates included Henry Frye, a Black scholar who would be elected to the N.C. Supreme Court in 1984.

Henry E. Frye, first Black North Carolina Supreme Court Justice, was a '59 law grad.

1960 Jim Hickey became the new football coach following the death of Coach Tatum. Don Skakle, who would become a legend in tennis coaching history, took over the netters' program. Student body musical preferences seemed a mixed bag as styles were changing: Duke Ellington and Count Basie came, as did Ray Charles and the Kingston Trio; Fats Domino had played here in 1959.

1961 Student leaders: Jim Smalley (*Yack* and student government), Howard Holderness (Honor Council), Ward Purrington (Student Council), and Jonathan Yardley (*DTH* editor). Tennis: 14 and 1.

1962 Soon-to-be Olympic basketball guard Larry Brown was elected Junior Class VP; Julius Chambers made Law Review; and everything on campus was suddenly Madras, the latest style. Roundballers suffered through an 8-8 regular season. President Kennedy spoke at University Day 1961 (Ed. note: See his speech and the essay by Terry Sanford), and the Isley Brothers came to town with a new dance craze: the "Twist." Dr. Frank Graham was a member of the Atomic Energy Commission and a consultant to the United Nations.

1963 "The only thing he's not yet learned is how to walk on water." That's how soph basketball sensation Billy "The Kid" Cunningham was described, and his 22.7 points per game and incredible 16 rebounds per game average bore it out. His teammates Charlie Shaffer and Larry Brown held student government offices, as did Bill Aycock II and Rufus Edmisten (the thin, handsome Chaplain of the SGA). Nine *Tar Heel* writers were assigned to cover civil rights activities in Oxford, Mississippi (Ed. note: For related article, see essay by Karen Parker). Tar Heel Larry Henry, who had never raced competitively until he came to UNC, finished first in a field of 68 to claim top ACC distance running honors. He did so *barefoot.* Music concerts: Joan Baez, Lester Flatt and Earl Scruggs.

1964 "Griselda," an eight-week-old pig, was unsuccessful in her bid for Student Body Secretary. 'Heels win Gator Bowl, 35-0, thanks to Ken Willard and Chris Harburger. Malcolm X, national Black Muslim leader, appeared in a Memorial Hall debate with Floyd McKissick, a Durham attorney. Music: Louis Armstrong and the Shirelles. If the *Yack* was scented, this year's smell would be English

"Billy C.," the "Kangaroo Kid," was the great early prize of the Dean Smith Era. Cunningham rewrote the Book on Rebounding and Scoring.

Leather Astronauts Wally Schirra, Gordon Cooper and Alan Shepard were among the first of dozens of astronauts who would receive pre-orbital training from Tony Jenzano and the Morehead Planetarium staff. Students, 10,889 of them, invaded campus in the fall—an increase of almost 1,000 over last year's record number. Many students had to live in ward-like settings in former study rooms and t.v. lounges because of the severe shortage of dorm rooms.

1965 Paul Sharp became Chancellor; the "peace symbol" was born; and the student body danced to the music of Elvis, the Four Seasons, and the Beatles. Ken Willard and Eddie Kessler could not play baseball in the spring because each had signed a pro football contract.

1966 A group of students walked 140 miles for charity; Woody Allen came to campus; UNC had a Black cheerleader for the first time; and the baseball team finished fourth in the NCAA. The University and her young president, William Friday, faced one of their toughest tests of faith ever, for this was the critical year of the infamous "Speaker Ban" controversy. In 1963 the General Assembly enacted that law and thereby prohibited speeches on the campuses of State-supported schools (e.g., UNC) by "known Communists," persons advocating the overthrow of the U.S. or N.C. Constitutions, or persons who pleaded the 5th Amendment in hearings on subversive organizations or activities.

On the night of February 24, 1966, more than 1,000 UNC students protested the Speaker Ban by staging an orderly walk to the home of President Friday, who himself had spent three years fighting the ruling. Three weeks later Communist Herbert Aptheker spoke to 2,000 UNC students from a sidewalk just beyond the Franklin Street wall, knowing that if he spoke from inside that wall, he would have been arrested. Finally, in 1968, a three-judge federal court in Greensboro struck down the Speaker Ban Law as unconstitutional. To many observers, it had been the state's darkest hour.

1967 The campus was filled with "flower children," not to be confused with the "flower ladies" on Franklin Street. Hundreds voted for Bill Cocke as "Ugliest Man on Campus." Bill Dooley's football squad goes 2 and 8, which was not indicative of the fine play of Danny Talbott, Jeff Beaver and others. Phil Riker made the Olympic swim team. And many said that this was Carolina's greatest basketball team: Lewis, Miller, Clark, Bunting, Gauntlett, Grubar, Brown, Tuttle and "Hatchet" Mirken (Ed. note: See essay by Charles Scott).

1968 Tar Heel students did anything they could, reasonable and unreasonable, to raise money for charity. Most fun charity project: Wooten Lamm led a contingency of students who covered themselves with mud. Carolina Forum brought Senators Hubert Humphrey, Barry Goldwater and Teddy Kennedy to campus. Hundreds stood in line at 6:00 AM to get tickets to the basketball game against Duke. Charlie Scott, Larry Miller & Company did not disappoint them.

1969 "The times, they are a changin'," said the songwriter, and 1969 was a different sort of year. Many students sported beards—a new look—and bluejeans. "Visitation," an awkward trial program that allowed females to visit male dorm rooms, was begun. The Beatles and Bob Dylan sang music students couldn't dance to. Joan Baez came to campus in support of striking food service workers, but before speaking she insisted that the American flag be removed from the stage. Richard Nixon came to campus, and while the popular politician was speaking to hundreds of students, campus policemen had a field day passing out parking tickets. Howard Lee was elected Mayor of Chapel Hill. So many students voiced concerns about the curriculum (i.e., some classes were too tough) that the University inaugurated the "Experimental College" program. Three Frank Porter Graham awards were given to student activists. The only thing normal about 1969 was the basketball team: They beat everybody in sight.

Pulitzer Prize-winner Jeff MacNelly, class of 1969, hammered home a lot of points with his classic political barbs and "Shoe" cartoons of the seventies and eighties.

1970 "Hippies" appeared in bell-bottom jeans—barefoot, braless, bearded. Coeds had long, straight hair; when not in Levis, they wore mini-skirts. Would-be Pulitzer Prize winner Jeff MacNelly ("Shoe") graced the publications with his creative cartoons. Students stayed out of classes to protest the presence of U.S. troops in Cambodia. Charlie Scott won a Frank Porter Graham award. The Association of Women Students sponsored seminars on "The Feminine Mystique." Don McCauley rushed for five touchdowns and 279 yards in the victory over Duke; he set an NCAA record with 1,720 yards rushing that season. A group of "conservative" students asked Chancellor Sitterson to discontinue funding of the *Tar Heel,* but the newspaper continued to win national awards for excellence as it celebrated its "78th Year of Editorial Freedom."

1971 Strangest *Yack* of all; published in two volumes with no text except a few quotes and captions. Students were driving vans decorated with paintings of sunsets and bumper stickers bearing serious political messages. Campus speakers: Jane Fonda and William F. Buckley. Bill Chamberlain, Dennis Wuycik and George Karl took over where Scott, Miller and Clark left off.

1972 Entertainment: Roberta Flack, the Nitty Gritty Dirt Band, the Byrds, the Supremes, and John Denver. Speakers: Norman Mailer and Ralph Nader. Students not wearing Topsiders were seen in sandals. Football team went 9-1 before losing in the Gator Bowl. Basketball: Fourth ACC and Eastern Regional crowns in six seasons; 29-5 record included wins over three international teams.

1973 Entertainment and speakers: James Taylor, Seals & Croft, Beach Boys ("Fun, Fun, Fun"), Jack Anderson ("Snoopy, Snoopy, Snoopy"), and Dick Gregory. Richard Epps was elected Student Body President. Coeds wore jeans; dresses were definitely *out* in 1973.

. . . a brief period of discrimination. . .

1974 Nine ZBT's wore boxer shorts in their *Yack* group photo. Sensational Tony Waldrop was ACC Athlete of the Year (Ed. note: See essay by A.J. Carr), and Bobby Jones led a world-class b'ball team. Speakers: Sam Ervin, Jr., David Brinkley, Bobby Seale, George McGovern, Gloria Steinem, and Jane Fonda (again). Entertainment: B.B. King, Judy Collins, Pointer Sisters, Sha Na Na, and Earth, Wind & Fire. There was a Black Arts Festival, a women's festival entitled "Multiple Choices," and female leadership of publications (*DTH:* Susan Miller, *Yack:* Martha Farlow).

"The Dean of Southern Sportswriters," Furman Bisher, with UNC Athletic Director Bill Cobey (right) in 1976.

1975 If you were away during Survival Symposium Week in March, perhaps you got back for Sexual Relationships Week. Loads of speakers that year: Angela Davis, Ralph Nader, Bernadette Devlin, Caesar Chavez, Stokely Carmichael, Admiral Elmo Zumwalt Tom Wolfe (not the UNC '20 novelist), Julian Bond, Eugene McCarthy, Rev. Ralph Abernathy and William Kuntsler. Student Body President: Marcus Williams. Entertainment: Phil Ford and friends made monkeys out of the Wolfpack and David Thompson (the defending NCAA champs), with Freshman Phil making a *Sports Illustrated* cover. Music: Linda Ronstadt, Gordon Lightfoot, Earl Scruggs, Kris Kristofferson and Rita Coolidge.

1976 Mike Voight rushed for 1,407 yards on the gridiron, including 261 yards in the wildest, wooliest Dook-Carolina game ever played. His two-point conversion iced it for the 'Heels, 39-38. Mitch Kupchak led a great 25-4 team, and he, Walter Davis, Phil Ford and Tommy LaGarde made Dean Smith/Bill Guthridge's Gold Medal Olympic Basketball team. Ford taught John Kuester how to land in fans' laps without hurting self or fans, but Kuester wiped out eight photographers while practicing his moves. Popular professor Bernard Boyd died in the fall. Mohammed Ali and Jeff MacNelly spoke, Lily Tomlin entertained. A Native American group was formed, as was the Neo-Hedonist Society. *DTH* sent reporters to Washington to interview Senator Jesse Helms.

Hugh Morton

The undisputed Gentleman of Basketball, Bobby Jones (# 34) of Charlotte outleaps the great David Thompson.

1977 Marquette squeaked by the injury-plagued 'Heels in the NCAA championship game, but Dudley Bradley and Mike O'Koren filed notice that they would be heard from the next season. *Yack* showed us a side of student life we could've lived without: a young man mooning. Two male students were shown embracing, perhaps during the Southeastern Gay Conference. A topless coed and marijuana being smoked—give us a break. Students protested the appearance of William Colby, former CIA Director. There was a B-1 Bomber Vigil; the protest of Senator Ervin's anti-ERA position by women students; and a visit by William Shatner ("Beam Lefty Driesell up, Scotty.)

1978 Phil Ford was NCAA Player of the Year, and thousands stayed late to give him a 10-minute standing ovation after he destroyed Duke in Carmichael. Speakers: Charles Kuralt, Tom Wicker, Jeff MacNelly, Bella Abzug, Arlo Guthrie. William F. Buckley taped his "Firing Line" program with Senator Ervin at Carolina Symposium. Toughest battle of the decade ended May 12th when Board of Governors Chairman William Johnson announced settlement of the prolonged desegregation case.

Journalist Tom Wicker

1979 Andy Griffith addressed a huge University Day audience. Orange County voted "yes" to liquor-by-the-drink. Two hundred students marched on South Building to protest several issues involving Blacks. Student Government Association provided funds to Carolina Gay Association. Paul Green Theatre opened. Speakers: Martin Luther King, Sr. and Madalyn Murray O'Hair. Incoming freshmen posted SAT score average of 1,063. Campus police issued 65,000 parking tickets in 1979 alone.

1980 Both "Famous Amos" Lawrence and Kelvin Bryant rushed for more than 1,000 yards that season, and together they scampered and bulldozed their way to 342 yards in the 44-21 win over Duke. The Iran Hostage Crisis evoked latent patriotism on campus, but at the same time students protested the revival of military draft registration. Joe Buckner founded UNC's Rape and Assault Prevention Escorts group. Speakers: Coretta King, Andrew Young, Pat Paulsen, Arthur Laffer, and Robert F. Kennedy, Jr. Entertainers: Sister Sledge and Doc and Merle Watson. *Mademoiselle* magazine visited UNC in search of models.

Decked out in "Air Jordan" clothing, Jack Morton of Raleigh (UNC class of 2000) poses with MJ.

Hugh Morton

1981 Lawrence Taylor was the top draft pick of the New York Giants. Carolina lost its #1 high school basketball prospect when Anthony Jones chose Georgetown, but the state's top player, Buzz Peterson, enrolled in September along with a player who had difficulty making the team at Laney High School in Wilmington. So how come four years later we couldn't buy Air Petersons? Speakers: G. Gordon Liddy, Jessie Jackson, Ben Chavis. Bumper Sticker of the year: "Virginia is for Losers," as Al Wood and Company routed Ralph in the Final Four. On April 30th football star Steve Streater endured a paralyzing auto accident (Ed. note: See Jill Leiber's *Sports Illustrated* excerpt). Six months later Kelvin Bryant scored six touchdowns against East Carolina—and then presented the ball to a beaming Streater (seated in a wheelchair next to the end zone). Ethan Horton and Bryant later led UNC to victory at the fog-enshrouded Gator Bowl.

1982 They measured the trash on Franklin Street in terms of Dumpstersfull (new word) following the all-night celebration of the NCAA championship victory over Georgetown (Ed. note: See Curry Kirkpatrick's essay). Worthy scored 28, Perkins 10, Jordan 16, and Chris Brust one ("Hey, it was an important free throw, right?") in the 63-62 win.

Women's soccer: NAIA champs; Lacrosse: NCAA champs; World Peace March; Carolina Students for Life protested abortion; and Interior Secretary James Watt was hanged in effigy.

1983 'Heels played Duke under portable lights in Kenan Stadium; Tyrone Anthony and Mr. Sue Walsh (i.e., Scott Stankavage) led the way to a 34-27 win. Check this list of UNC teams that won ACC championships: women's soccer, basketball, volleyball, and swimming; men's baseball, golf, and swimming. The basketball team won 28 games thanks to Jordan, Perkins, Peterson, Doherty, Martin, Hale, and giant freshman Brad Daugherty.

1984 Pictured in the *Yack:* a KKK march; a Die-In calling for nuclear disarmament (Participants lay down on brick walks and had their bodies outlined in chalk); a Death Vigil for Gary Hutchins; and an anti-Klan rally. Freshmen Kenny Smith, Joe Wolf and Dave Popson helped lead roundballers to 28 wins. Speakers: Louis Harris (UNC grad turned Famous Pollster), Shirley Chisholm, Crystal Lee Sutton (about whom "Norma Rae" was filmed), Walter Mondale, Gary Hart, and Jessie Jackson.

1985 This is a difficult yearbook to follow because the editors arranged everything alphabetically, beginning with such subjects as "Abortion" and "AIDS." Carmichael Auditorium was no longer "Blue Heaven" following the Clemson game, but—wait!—it was decided later that a second "Last Game in Carmichael" would be played against State on January 4, 1986. Eddie Murphy's concert sold out in March. Black female Patricia Wallace was elected Student Body President. And Jeff Lebo enrolled in September, 1985. That made many people happy.

1986 You *knew* he had something up his sleeve. Yes, even though his team had just lost, Jim Valvano—recognizing that it was only a game—made the last basket in Carmichael. The Dean E. Smith Center opened on January 18th (black tie affair the night before) with a rousing romp of Duke, 95-92. It was Steve Hale's finest performance. The year belonged to Coach Smith and President Friday as thousands thanked both of them for their untiring dedication to and love for the University. "Skipper" Bowles watched from his wheelchair as his grandson threw up the first ball in the new arena. (Brad Daugherty outjumped Mark Alarie by three feet.) On University Day the entire campus and village turned out to bid farewell to "retiring" President Friday—a man who will surely be working a 12-hour day at age 120! C.D. Spangler, who (unlike Friday) had the common sense to get his undergraduate degree at Carolina, became the new President of the then 16-campus University. And students were still students in 1986: they protested apartheid, nuclear weapons, the lack of campus facilities for the handicapped, and the all-female dance show at a place called "Rascals."

1987 Two hundred three years after William Sharpe of Rowan County introduced in the Legislature a bill (which was defeated) to charter "the North Carolina University," a 6'9" freshman from Virginia—Herman Reid, Jr.,—enrolled at the storied institution. The way he was treated—moreover, the way *all* students were treated in 1987—was proof that the University experiment had succeeded. The pictures proved it, for there—under tall pines and inside ivy-covered dorms, classroom buildings, and labs—young men and women from nearly every state in the nation pursued together the search for Truth. Black, white, Native American, Hispanic, Oriental, female, male, gay, liberal, conservative, short and tall—all were welcomed and all were treated with dignity and respect. It was not as if *all* were looked up to with the same kind of adoring respect afforded Herman Reid, Jr., but it was clear that—finally—all women and men were treated as equals.

Edward Kidder Graham said it best in 1912: "Measured in terms of the profound realities for which she stands, judged on a national basis, and by national standards, I believe that the University of North Carolina is the best product of her civilization that North Carolina has to show to the world."

Hugh Morton

"Skipper" Bowles described this as "my all-time favorite photo of myself"—taken in Philadelphia at the NCAA championship game of 1981.

Prior to 1903 a swampy, undistinguished area was used as a pasture by local residents. Professor W.C. Coker planned and planted trees, shrubs, vines and flowering vegetation for the enjoyment of many generations. Walkways, some trellis-covered, enhance a stroll through the arboretum.

KENAN STADIUM

by Sibyl Goerch Powe

Kenan Stadium is like no other stadium in the world, having been set down in a natural valley and framed all around with tall pines and hardwoods. Each Saturday during football season, the colors of the trees change dramatically. At the first game in September, shades of green seem to envelop the gleaming white stands. In late September soft reds and yellows begin recoloring those trees around the rim. By October there are brilliant splashes among the pines and cedars as maples and oaks turn scarlet, sweetgums deepen purple, and hickories shine like gold. Starting with the neatly striped turf and looking up at the white stands, then at the colorful trees, and last at the deep blue sky, the panorama you see is as vast as it is beautiful. Even in bad weather, when winds whip through the trees or rain spatters against the spectators' gaily colored umbrellas, Kenan Stadium is a magnificent tribute to man and nature.

It was built in 1927, and was a gift to the school from William Rand Kenan, Jr., class of 1894. Upon hearing that some alumni were trying to raise money to build a new athletic field, he wrote the University that he would be happy to pay for the field, the bleachers, and everything else needed, upon one condition—that it would be named as a memorial to his parents.

It was dedicated with great ceremony on a glorious Thanksgiving Day, November 24, 1927, when Carolina's football team played its arch rival, the University of Virginia, and beat them 14-13. Mr. and Mrs. William Rand Kenan, Jr. brought their friends, Mr. and Mrs. John Motley Morehead, down from New York for the occasion in the Kenans' own private railway car (which had to be parked on a siding over in Durham because the track didn't go all the way to Chapel Hill). The Kenans' long-time friend, John Sprunt Hill, made the formal presentation speech, and Governor A.W. McLean accepted the memorial gift in behalf of the Trustees and the State. The splendid stadium, the brilliant day, the exultant fans, and the pageantry of the presentation of the munificent Kenan gift created unforgettable images for everyone who attended the premiere event. It also marked the beginning of "big-time football" at Chapel Hill.

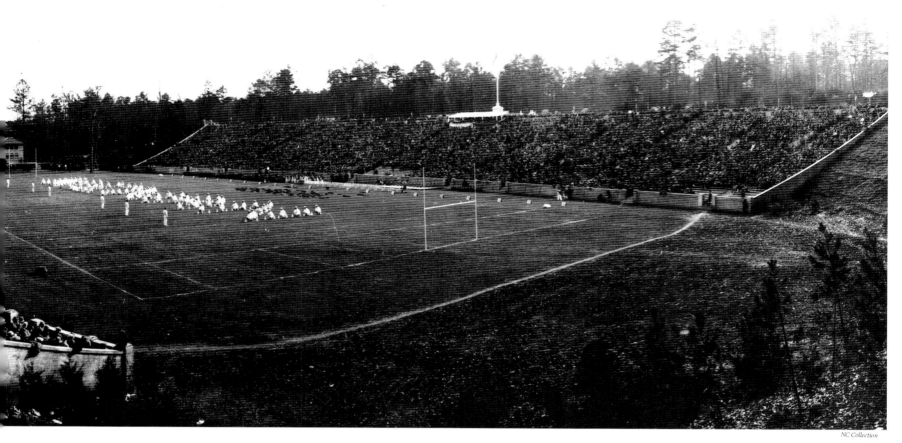

Kenan Stadium, one of the world's most glorious sporting arenas, was dedicated on Thanksgiving Day, 1927.

Before TV took the game of football out of the stadium and put it into millions of living rooms, only those who actually went to the games could really know the thrill of those Saturday afternoons. Young and old alike streamed into the bleachers, bringing along sun visors, laprobes, seat cushions, cowbells, and binoculars. Even the little boys who evaded the ticket-takers and perched in tall treetops to watch the game became part of the scene.

There was always a band playing um-pah-pah marches, tall-hatted drum majors prancing ahead, twirling batons tossed high by the majorettes, and cheerleaders stirring the crowd on to yell, "Gimme a C, Gimme an A, Gimme an R. . ." There were coeds adorned with huge white chrysanthemums, and fans waving pennants on long, pointed sticks. Peddlers hawked popcorn, peanuts and drinks: "Ice cold Coke! Only a dime!"

An imposing official in black and white knickers broke up a touch football game on the field; a stray dog from town chased the mascot, old Rameses, and the loud speaker sputtered and crackled and popped: "Yackety Yack, Ray Ray, Yackety Yack, Rah, Rah!"

Then blue-jerseyed players ran single-file on the field; the "Star Spangled Banner" brought fans to their feet; a toss of the coin and the ball was kicked down field; drums rolled like thunder; and Tar Heel fans shrieked: "Let's go-o-o-o, Carolina!"

William Rand Kenan, Jr., class of 1894, was one of the University's most generous benefactors during the school's first 200 years.

REMEMBERING "DR. FRANK"

by Tom Wicker

The Rev. Vance Barron recalled at the funeral of Dr. Frank Porter Graham that "'Dr. Frank' once told me that there cannot be anything higher in life than the revelation that God is love." It was that gentle heart, that loving spirit, far more than his great achievements, that made Frank Graham's life so radiant. In good times and bad, in theory and in fact, in word and deed, he loved his fellow man and in that way best loved his God.

As a history teacher the memory of whose lectures still delights an older generation of students; as the president who made the University into the light of the South in the hard days of the nineteen-thirties and forties; as a U.S. Senator ultimately defeated in a bitter racist campaign; as one of those who began the modern civil rights movement under President Truman; and in his last active years as a tireless international servant of the United Nations—in all these different and usually thankless tasks, his gentleness never deserted him, the love in his heart never withered. He was, Wayne Morse once said, "the most Christlike man I've ever known."

He was nevertheless a hard fighter. When one of his faculty was accused of the heinous crime of lunching with a Black man, Dr. Frank calmly told the trustees, "If Professor Erickson has to go on a charge of eating with another human being, then I will have to go first." As a magazine writer commented at about that time, Frank Graham has planted "one foot firmly on the Sermon on the Mount and the other on the Bill of Rights."

Still, it was not his deeds nor his strength that most distinguished Dr. Frank. He could salve a student's troubled spirit with a smile and lift men's hearts by example. In the meanest trial of his life, his spirit held him steady and a whole generation of North Carolinians could learn from him what was meant by courage under fire and charity of the soul.

That was in 1950, when he ran for the Senate seat to which he had been appointed by Governor Kerr Scott. In the Democratic primary, despite repeated charges that he was somehow pro-Communist and unpatriotic, Dr. Frank got more votes than anyone up to then had received for any state office—but with three candidates in the race, he just failed to win a majority. In the runoff, the attack shifted to the worst kind of racist charges, and he was defeated. On the race question as on the human question, Frank Graham was ahead of his time.

Yet, he never struck back with lies and innuendo of his own, nor later denounced the men who had slandered him. Dr. Frank did not make the common, fatal error of public men—he never believed his cause was so precious, his victory so necessary, that they could justify any tactic or any means.

So he could stand in the U.S. Senate as he was about to leave it and deliver a farewell address unmarked by bitterness, infused with a vision of America and of humankind unaltered by his ordeal: "In this America of our struggles and our hopes," he said, "the least of these our brethren has the freedom to struggle for freedom; where the answer to error is not terror, the respect for the past is not reaction and the hope of the future is not revolution; where the integrity of simple people is beyond price and the daily toil of millions is above pomp and power; where the majority is without tyranny, and the minority without fear, and all people have hope."

The hard men, the practical men, the so-called realists will never share or know that vision. But then they will never even know that, whatever the momentary situation, they can win nothing that matters; or that in the everlasting verities of the heart, Frank Graham never lost.

"Dr. Frank," shown here in a 1939 shot taken in his backyard, achieved more by age 21 than most men accomplish in a lifetime.

THE ARCHITECT AND SPIRITUAL FATHER OF THE UNIVERSITY

by Dr. Arnold K. King

I knew Frank Graham from the time I was a freshman at Chapel Hill in 1919 until his death in 1972. He was an authentic genius, perhaps the only one that this state has produced in this century. He was the architect and spiritual father of the greatest university of its kind in the United States.

In his senior year at Carolina (1909) he was president of his class, secretary of Phi Beta Kappa, editor of the *Yackety Yack,* editor-in-chief of the *Daily Tar Heel,* president of the YMCA, and head cheerleader. That gives you just a hint of the versatility of Dr. Frank. He went on to study law here, to teach high school English in Raleigh for a couple of years, and to do graduate study in history at Columbia University, where he received his master's degree in 1915. From that time until he became a U.S. Senator in 1949, he was associated with this institution.

By 1930, the year he was elected the eleventh president of the University, it was evident to all that Frank Graham was a rare and unusual person, selfless, visionary, humane, fearless, warm-hearted, and intellectually honest. He was almost too good to be true. People were drawn to him from all walks of life. His unswerving devotion to his conception of right and justice frequently taxed the patience of both his friends and his antagonists, but no one ever questioned his character.

A TRIBUTE TO CHAPEL HILL

by Frank Porter Graham

In Chapel Hill among a friendly folk, this old University, the first state University to open its doors, stands on a hill set in the midst of beautiful forests under the skies that give their color and their charm to the life of youth gathered here. Traditions grow here with the ivy on the historic buildings and the moss on the ancient oaks. Friendships form here for the human pilgrimage. There is music in the air of the place. To the artist's touch flowers grow beautifully from the soil and plays come simply from the life of the people. Above the traffic of the hour, church spires reach toward the life of the spirit. Into this life, with its ideals, failures, and high courage, comes youth with his body and his mind, his hopes and his dreams. Scholars muster here the intellectual and spiritual resources of the race for the development of the whole personality of the poorest boy, and would make the University of North Carolina a stronghold of liberal learning with outposts of research along all the frontiers of the world. Great teachers on this hill kindle the fires that burn for him and light up the heavens of the commonwealth with the hopes of light and liberty for all mankind.

"Silent Sam"

THE TIN CAN WAS A PALACE, TOO

by Furman Bisher

      I am proud to watch a Carolina team play now, football or basketball, but as a sports writer I have to at least "appear" to be "assuming a posture of neutrality." I look at that palace—the Dean E. Smith Center—and I apologize to all the trees they cut down to build it. I assure you that none of them entering those doors gets half the pleasure I got out of the Tin Can. If you're too young to know of the Tin Can, go ask your grandpa. As far as I was concerned, it was the grandest palace I ever saw. You have to remember I came from Denton, where palaces are rare.

      When I'm at the Smith Center I can't help but think back to days of eating in Swain Hall. I learned a lot about "service" there watching busboys who were not above dealing with the refuse left by their fellow man. Out of this platoon of young servants came some of our glorious leaders: One became Governor and later U. S. Senator, two were football stars, one became an admiral, another president of a great corporation, and finally there was the State Senator—almost elected Governor—who was largely responsible for the Dean E. Smith Center's existence. I am proud to call these classmates my friends: Sanford, Burnette, Kline, Bass and Bowles.

The "Tin Can" was the site of the Senior Ball of 1937.

A COMMUNITY OF GIVERS

by Marie Watters Colton

I grew up in Chapel Hill in the years just prior to and during World War II. It was a village where all its citizens—from doctors and lawyers to merchants and city workers—were in some way involved in the University. My high school teachers were often prominent members of the University faculty; my schoolmates were their offspring.

During those formative years I was shocked by the experience of having a schoolmate indicted and tried as a Communist. I was thrilled as a member of the Carolina Political Union when Senator Harry Truman and Mrs. Eleanor Roosevelt were among those who accepted our invitation to visit the campus. I was stimulated by knowing and watching many distinguished members of the community as they carried out exciting plans. Dr. Benjamin Swalin established the first state-sponsored symphony orchestra. Dr. Rhoulac Hamilton made the Southern Historical Collection a first-rate repository of archival material. Paul Green was crafting a new drama form that would change our perspective on history, and Dr. Albert Coates was developing his fledgling Institute of Government, where I was employed as a statistician the summer after my high school graduation.

Dr. Frank Graham presided over the University with graciousness and integrity, helping lead it to a preeminent position among the nation's universities. "Dr. Frank," of course, would later go on to the U.S. Senate and to a distinguished career at the United Nations.

There were many other people in that small, intimate community who were making names for themselves far beyond the boundaries of the University. How could one not be affected by the dynamics of such a place? It was a time when ideas became actions—with the University serving as the "laboratory" for this chemistry. Part of the beauty of the University process is that it invites everyone—young and old alike—to participate in its quests and discoveries, and all who participate are changed, presumably for the better. For me, that process led to a career in government based on the conviction that we are each here to make the world a better place for the next generation.

The University, then as now, was often the catalyst for critical political and social change in the land. From William R. Davie and James K. Polk to Frank Porter Graham, William C. Friday, Christopher Fordham and C.D. Spangler, the University has provided a rich legacy of service to community.

The Chapel Hill and University community I grew up in was, and still is, a unified body of "givers"—men and women who are genuinely willing to sacrifice "self" for the good of the corporate body. That is a precious heritage to pass on to the students and faculty of tomorrow. And to those who gave so that I might learn such a lesson, thank you.

NC Collection

Mrs. Eleanor Roosevelt is flanked on the Chapel Hill stage by (left to right) Chancellor Robert B. House, John Sprunt Hill and President Frank Porter Graham.

Hugh Morton

The most popular poplar in the world was named for the University's founder, William R. Davie.

CHAPEL HILL: A PLACE OF ROMANCE

by Grace R. Hamrick

My first date as a student in the fall of 1939 was tall and handsome, a true Carolina gentleman in every sense of the word. When he arrived at my dorm (known then as No. 2 and now as McIver), he pinned a single rose on my Peter Pan collar. This made a big hit with the girls in the lobby as they watched, and it made me feel very special.

He was in his Sunday-best suit (and tie!) with shiny wing-tip shoes, and he treated me to a movie and, afterwards, to Viennese coffee and pastries at Danziger's. I'm sure he stretched his budget since most of us received an allowance of only $4 to $5 a week. We hummed to the tunes on the nickelodeon, and even today memories go back when I hear "Sunrise Serenade," "Moon River," "Pennies From Heaven," "Sentimental Journey" and "Pennsylvania Six-Five Thousand."

We saved enough time before my 11 p.m. check-in to walk to Graham Memorial for a "mixer," which was a party and not something to drink.

Through the years we have remained good friends. Each Christmas our families exchange notes and news. Thankfully, each of us has been happily married (to the same spouse) for more than 40 years—I to the fellow student to whom he introduced me, Rush Hamrick, Jr.

My second date was a dashing pre-med student who seemingly had his manners as polished as his shoes. We left the dorm, strolled through the arboretum and came to a bench near the Old Well. It was a gorgeous, moonlit night. We thought we would get to know each other better—through conversation, that is—but as it turned out, he wanted more than I expected to give. His pre-med studies of the female anatomy must have needed refreshing, but I was neither his cadaver nor practice person.

I was startled and couldn't believe what was happening. I'll never forget the struggle nor the disappointment of this wrestling match under the Davie Poplar, and even though I exited unscathed, I was humiliated and embarrassed. A week or so later he called to invite me to a movie, but I "had other plans."

Reflecting on that incident, I realize that I learned a great deal that night. Both of us were growing and being tested, which is what the college experience is all about.

When I think of other dates at Carolina I can't help but think of the "Tin Can," that make-shift building built in 1923 to "temporarily" house basketball, boxing, wrestling, indoor track and some of the greatest dances held anywhere. Before being torn down in 1977 to make way for Fetzer Gym, it was one of recorded history's oldest "temporary" buildings. Dating there was always fun. How fond are the memories of learning the "big apple" there, and dancing to Larry Clinton and the Dipsy Doodlers, Jan Savit, Dean Hudson, Al Donahue and Bubbles Becker, Jimmy Lunceford, Tommy Dorsey, Frank Sinatra, Glen Gray and the Casa Lomans, and Kay Kyser. Skipper Bowles was a band leader favorite on campus at that time, which may explain in part why he worked so hard to raise funds for the new Smith Center. Skipper appreciated the full meaning of the term "Student Activities Center," because that's what the Tin Can had been for us.

YOUR HEART IS FOREVER AT HOME HERE

by Kays Gary

It is the place of immortality; the place where we are forever young.

It is the place, more than any other, where we became what we are and it is, perhaps, the greatest legacy we leave for sons and daughters.

Chapel Hill.

The University of North Carolina.

The temple of our spirit. . .

Where we discovered we ARE somebody. . .

Thanks to the incredible wizardry of teachers and counselors.

And the mines of truth are ever deep and waiting with treasures to enrich us all in the ways that matter most.

Chapel Hill.

The University of North Carolina.

Surely it was not forever Spring there. Or Autumn.

But those are the images memories hold.

And the rain. Walking in the rain. Alone. Or with someone. A friend. Or love.

There was an exuberant oneness in Kenan on Saturdays, in Memorial Hall at Dorsey-Sinatra concerts, in dorm or frat house bull sessions, in the daily "Y Court" assemblies and in the village itself—ever changing but staying the same in people-ness.

We gloried, even, with the on-campus appearances of politicians of every stripe, proponents of elitist political philosophies and social renegades. We found our voices among them. Our tested beliefs grew stronger.

They were, after all, beliefs pronounced in the Constitution of the United States of America only a handful of years before our founders gathered beneath Davie Poplar.

Lux Veritas.

And truth can be served only by men free to pursue it.

Chapel Hill.

The University of North Carolina.

Many of us were poor. But our University has always known that the poor can have eager minds and dreams to know and grow, to live and give and somehow add to the sum of good. And so many of the once-poor are the richest among us. Giving now. Not so much in gratitude as in conviction that the University is the best investment one can make in North Carolina's future.

To the new student we would suggest that the future is now and even now can be enjoyed as it will be forever after. So enjoy. Your roommate may be a United States Senator, a governor, a playwright, actor, doctor, scientist, artist, educator, financier, minister, musician Your friends will become all these and more and, for a lifetime, you will glory in them and, like as not, they in you.

You will never, ever, be friendless.

And your heart will forever have a home.

Chapel Hill.

The University of North Carolina.

Hugh Morton

"Blue Eyes" Frank Sinatra (right) crooned to the delight of coeds at the May Frolics spring dance in 1942. Big band leader Tommy Dorsey performs with Chuck Lowrey and Jo Stafford; on the left is drumming great Buddy Rich.

Poet Robert Frost tiptoed into many UNC classrooms in the 1950's.

CAROLINA'S CONTRIBUTION
TO WORLD WAR II

by Orville B. Campbell

Few people remember the tremendous contribution that the University made to the World War II war effort from Chapel Hill.

Wise UNC administrators like Frank Graham and Billy Carmichael, Jr., as early as May 1940, were very much aware that a war was in the offing that would involve most of the world powers. Hitler was on the move in Europe. A telegram was sent to Washington by Graham and Carmichael offering the entire University facilities to the U.S. government with no strings attached. The Civil Aeronautics Authority director at the time, Nolan Ryan, declared the Horace Williams Airport to be the finest college airport in the nation. The CAA program on the campus, two years before the Japanese attack on Pearl Harbor, had trained more than 60 student pilots.

UNC students, who would be in battle very shortly, showed much less interest about a possible war than Graham or Carmichael or many other concerned faculty members.

When it was announced on Feb. 27, 1942, that UNC had been selected for the location of a U.S. Navy Pre-Flight School, tranquil Chapel Hill was never the same until the war had ended.

There were to be four Pre-Flight Schools where future Navy and Marine pilots would go through the "most intensive, rigorous, and comprehensive program of physical and mental training that the world has ever seen." More than 70 colleges and universities applied to be one of those four schools.

The University of Iowa, representing the Midwest, was the first Pre-Flight School selected; St. Mary's College in California and the University of Georgia were chosen to represent the West and South. The odds appeared to be against UNC after Georgia was selected, but through the personal contacts that Frank Graham had with President Franklin Roosevelt, Chapel Hill was selected as the fourth site. A fifth school was assigned at Del Monte, California in 1943 when the demand for pilots increased.

Alexander Hall became the administration building; Caldwell Hall and Manning Hall served as classroom space. Ten dormitories (Stacy, Graham, Everett, Aycock, Lewis, Mangum, Manly, Grimes, Ruffin and part of Alexander) were used to house naval personnel and cadets. Carr Dormitory was later used to house V-5 instructors participating in the indoctrination course.

Lenoir Hall served as the cadet dining hall, and almost all athletic facilities, including Woollen Gymnasium, Bowman Gray Swimming Pool, Kenan Stadium, Emerson and Fetzer Fields, Tin Can, tennis courts and other athletic fields were taken over by the Navy.

Navy cadet guards were on duty 24 hours a day at every entrance to facilities used by the Pre-Flight School. The cadets termed their quadrangle "hell's half acre." That was an excellent description. The program was so tough that about 25 percent of the cadets flunked out and were sent to other branches of service.

From where did these cadets come? Most of them were from Eastern schools like Princeton, Cornell, Williams, Amherst, Dartmouth, Yale, and Harvard, to name a few. They were the cream of the crop of young Americans getting ready for battle. A young naval officer by the name of Gerald Ford spent a few months in a cottage on Burlage Circle. Otto Graham, who was both an All-American football and basketball player at Northwestern, and Ted Williams, no credentials needed, were here for pre-flight training. Bear Bryant and hundreds of other college coaches served as instructors. The cadets were the finest group of young men ever assembled for any war. They arrived as typical college graduates, out of shape and wondering what their destiny might be. They left as tough as any Marine, ready for any danger that should lie ahead.

The first battalion arrived in May 1942, and the 75th battalion came aboard in mid-September 1945. Each battalion stayed for 12 weeks. Almost 25 percent of the cadets who became pilots from the first 25 battalions were killed in action. Cadets who trained in

The Pre-Flight School changed almost everything in Chapel Hill, including chow time in Lenoir Hall.

Chapel Hill were partly responsible for the success of the Navy at the Battle of the Coral Sea—one of the turning points of the war in the Pacific.

Where there is toughness there is always humor. One cadet exclaimed to a friend, "I think if I live through it, I'll be able to fly without wings."

What did the University directly contribute to the war? A total of 18,700 cadets were received for training. There were 1,220 officers, mostly military and physical training instructors, indoctrinated at Chapel Hill. Three hundred sixty French cadets arrived in May 1944 along with 78 French officers. Many Navy and Coast Guard officers came to Chapel Hill for a special two-week course of instruction in survival practices. Special training was also provided for many photographers who headed to the battle front to tell of the horrors of war.

Besides the 1,875 cadets on the base, 768 officers and 715 enlisted personnel were attached to the Pre-Flight School at any one time.

The first all-Black band in the Navy lived in the Hargraves Community Center on Roberson Street and proved to be a great morale builder to everyone at the base.

In the early months of the Pre-Flight School's existence several skirmishes occurred between cadets, students and townspeople. However, it was not long before a unified spirit and willingness of self-sacrifice brought almost complete cooperation.

What were the benefits to the University and the state? Chapel Hill and the entire South gained respect from those who trained here. Every dormitory that the Pre-Flight School used was re-built good as new. The present UNC infirmary was built by the Navy, as was Kessing Pool, the women's old gym, Navy Field and the Undergraduate admission's building, which is located across from the Forest Theater.

The road to the Horace Williams Airport, which is now known as Airport Road, was a dirt road that became paved. The facilities at Lenoir Hall were improved. The government, besides paying rent for the use of buildings and other space that might have been vacant for lack of students, spent at least $2 million for campus improvements that are still being used.

One can look back 45 years and remember that only half the road to the Raleigh-Durham Airport was paved. But, believe it or not, you could get to the Quonset hut airport then just about as quickly as you can today with the arrival of I-40 and the widening of N.C. 54.

The University grew to maturity during those Pre-Flight School days. Dr. Graham spent most of his time in Washington working directly with President Roosevelt, and Billy Carmichael, Jr. was acting President of the University. Bob House was before, during the war, and for many years afterwards the Chancellor at Chapel Hill. He still lives in that old home on Franklin Street, and he remembers the Pre-Flight days as happy memories during very difficult times.

Sally Sather

FROM CLYDE KING TO SUE WALSH

by A.J. Carr

Clyde King of Goldsboro went from a dorm room at Carolina to the dugout of Brooklyn in less than 24 hours.

Most college athletes only dream of getting *that* phone call. Clyde King of Goldsboro, a tall, gangling Carolina pitcher in 1945, didn't even do that. Deep down he held little hope of a career in baseball, and then he got *the* phone call—it came from Branch Rickey of the Dodgers. Within an hour—lugging a suitcase bearing a "Beat Dook" sticker on the side—King was hurriedly boarding a train for Brooklyn. Two days later the dream he never dreamed came true: He pitched in the first major league game he ever saw.

"I got the first two guys out before Mel Ott, who made the Hall of Fame, came to the plate. I don't need to tell you what Mel did to the ball," chuckled King.

It all happened so suddenly, but for the gentleman Tar Heel it marked the beginning of 43 consecutive years in professional baseball as a player, scout, field manager, general manager, and executive for the Dodgers, Giants, Braves, and Yankees. Mild-mannered with a studious demeanor, King has long been viewed as the Christian competitor, a symbol of good on and off the field. As a pitcher he won 14 games for the Dodgers in 1951, and that year he came out of the bullpen twice in one day and collected both pitching victories in a doubleheader. He holds the distinction of having retired Cardinal Hall-of-Famer Stan Musial seven times in a row. Later, in King's three years as general manager, the Yankees averaged 92 victories per season.

But for all the big hats he has worn, he has never gotten big-headed. When time has permitted, he has stopped by Chapel Hill to help coach Carolina's pitchers. Said King's lovely wife, Norma: "After 43 years Clyde still loves to go to the ball park."

Little Jim Beatty, at 5'4" and 126 pounds, turned into the biggest man of all in track and field during the early sixties. All heart and legs, Beatty gained the immutable distinction of being the first American to break the four-minute mile barrier indoors, striding to a world record of 3:58.9 in 1962. The Carolina speedster also set a world mark in the outdoor two-mile, then ran and won several political races.

In 1974 Morehead Scholar Tony Waldrop burst onto the scene like a blur. He ran nine straight sub-four-minute miles, setting a world record at 3:55.0, then improving to a personal best of 3:53.2. Waldrop's feats also included two national championship crowns in the mile and 1,000-yard distances, six ACC titles, and NCAA *academic* honors to boot.

In swimming, no one made a bigger (or smaller) splash than Sue Walsh—four times an All-American, 11 times a national champion, winner of 15 ACC titles, and holder of three American records. Somehow, she had enough energy left to make Phi Beta Kappa. After graduation, she became Sue Walsh Stankavage when she married former Tar Heel quarterback Scott Stankavage.

April Heinrichs was known for scooting around Chapel Hill on a moped and scooting around opponents on the soccer field. Quick and aggressive, Heinrichs earned All-America honors four times, set Tar Heel records for goals and assists, was named soccer's 1986 Female Athlete of the Year, and helped Carolina win three national titles. April was "Ms. October," an athlete Coach Anson Dorrance unabashedly called "one of the best women soccer players in the world."

Until Coach Willie Scroggs came along, lacrosse was thought of primarily as a northern game, or—as one scribe noted—a town in Wisconsin. Today lacrosse is a popular sport at Carolina. Scroggs quickly built powerhouse teams, gave traditional toughie Johns Hopkins the willies, and guided the Tar Heels to three national championships.

Jack Nicklaus, II came to Chapel Hill with a big name and then produced a golf game to match. "The Golden Cub" won the 1985 North-South Amateur, a prestigious title his father had also captured. But perhaps his finest hour came when he caddied for the elder Nicklaus at the 1986 Masters. In one of sports' great moments, young Jack advised the Old Master as to the perils of Augusta National's 18th green, and Nicklaus, Sr. followed his son's teaching and won yet another coveted green jacket. The scene thrilled multimillions via television.

Every March the crack of the batted ball is a melodic sound that helps make spring sing at Carolina. Coaches Bunn Hearn, Walter Rabb, and Mike Roberts have provided championship caliber teams and produced pro prospects—including three major league catchers—in the process.

UNC's Jim Beatty and Tony Waldrop set world records in the mile in 1962 and 1974, respectively.

Hugh Morton

UNC's "Golden Cub," Jack Nicklaus, Jr., with the Master.

Soccer star April Heinrichs was known as "The Female Pele" in Chapel Hill.

Lacross immortal:
Willie Scroggs

For a brief span in the eighties, B.J. Surhoff was "Mr. Baseball" at UNC. He was NCAA Player of the Year in 1985, the number one draft pick of the Milwaukee Brewers, two-time All-America, and two-time ACC Player of the Year. Surhoff, in short, could do it all—hit, run, throw, catch and sell peanuts. Though mostly a catcher, he played *eight* positions in high school and college.

Dwight Lowry and Scott Bradley—both major league catchers—were outstanding All-Americans at Carolina. Scott Bankhead, a Bulldog battler with a strong arm, posted a school record 24 wins against three losses, won 20 in a row during one stretch, earned a position on the U.S. Olympic team, and made it to the majors with Kansas City.

In tennis, Vic Seixas and Bitsy Grant left indelible marks at Carolina, then stroked their way to international acclaim. Tar Heel Freddie McNair also succeeded on the pro circuit, capturing a French Open doubles title with Sherwood Stewart, and UNC's Laura DuPont played well on the women's pro tour.

Finally, 134-pound C.D. Mock proved that you don't have to be named Jordan or Justice or J.R. to get respect in sports. Though he didn't perform before a national television audience, and though he didn't grapple to the tune of "I-Ziggy-Zoomba," Mock won the NCAA wrestling championship and the coveted Patterson Medal, the premier athletic award at UNC.

Sue Walsh, eight-time NCAA champion.

Carolina's golf program has turned out many champions, but to date the demand for tickets at Finley Golf Course is low...except when Michael Jordan's on the tee.

Many future major leaguers chewed their first tobacco in the shadow of the Bell Tower.

Tar Heel Jonathan Hall (no. 5) helped bring Carolina through a winning season in 1986.

Chip Henderson

It is easy to see where 50,000 or so Carolinians spend their Saturday afternoons in autumn.

Chancellor House was never without his harmonica—"my notes," he called them. He would pull out his "notes" at Board meetings and ball games, before church and after breakfast. He is shown here in 1952 playing to the delight of a Wilmington lad.

NOBLE SPIRITS

by William C. Friday

One of the major sources of joy and pleasure over these last thirty years has been the privilege I have had of working with men of quality, strength and dedication who have served as Chancellors of the University at Chapel Hill. Each is a different personality, each has a different set of qualifications. Yet, their common dedication is their uncommon commitment to the University and their love for this place. Each continues in service to the University today.

Robert House, acting upon Fred Weaver's recommendation, gave me my first appointment in the University. Over these years, I have seen this great spirit traveling across the state serving as the University's minister to everyone, speaking of the value of learning, religion, and hard work. Traveling with him to his many speaking assignments was instructive because he was a great story-teller and willingly shared his knowledge of the history of the University.

Once I asked him what our work hours were and he gave a prophetic answer: "There are no hours for us in the administration." Later, while riding the special train to New York for the Notre Dame game in Yankee Stadium, we met at daybreak in the last coach of the train for coffee he had fixed. The next hour we discussed the virtues of the single-wing formation! He loved the Scriptures, and during most of his years he has read the Bible, Shakespeare and other great literature during the early morning hours. In great measure, his unselfish devotion to this place made the national and international career of Frank Graham possible. He was always on the scene in Chapel Hill.

When his son, Robert, Jr., died I walked over to his house; he met me in the yard, embraced me with his powerful left arm, and a tear fell from his face. His great heart was in deep grief because Robert House loved his family dearly and lived and taught the high value of family togetherness. He is now in his nineties in his residence on Franklin Street, and that joyful heart and twinkling eye will greet you warmly when you visit him.

William Aycock and I have been friends and colleagues most of our working years. I knew of him initially as President of the Student Body at North Carolina State. While a student leader, he was confronted with serious problems in intercollegiate athletics, and his strong stand insisting on integrity in sports was the crowning glory of his term of office. He came home from World War II a decorated leader, and entered the University School of Law. For the next two years he led our study group and our class in scholarship. Inviting him to become Chancellor was, for me, a proud and confident decision because I knew of his great intellectual strength, his good humor, and his compassionate heart. Bill Aycock set high standards for himself, and he expected comparable levels of performance from those with whom he served. The quality of his mind and the depth of his courage were clearly evident in his Speaker Ban statements, his ERA position papers, his firmness with athletics, and his strong efforts with students, alumni, legislators and benefactors. He introduced long-range planning into administration processes to stabilize growth and development. And on each Christmas Eve he walked the wards of Memorial Hospital to bring a personal greeting to those confined there.

William Aycock has always been a teacher, and he has won every recognition and award the University gives for good teaching because he is the best. His compelling sense of public service, great energy, and boundless curiosity keep him in the middle of many activities today.

Chancellor William Aycock

Coming to Chapel Hill from Hiram College in Ohio, Paul Sharp followed William Aycock into the Chancellorship. This affable man and I spent a delightful day visiting Connemara, the home of Carl Sandburg, the great historian. We were there to deliver to Mr. Sandburg a special White House photograph and a personal letter from President Lyndon Johnson honoring the eminent American scholar on his birthday. Dr. Sharp did not remain with us very long before being called to the Presidency of Drake University, and he later served as President of the University of Oklahoma. Since his retirement he has lectured on university administration at home and abroad.

Carlyle Sitterson will always be gratefully remembered for his patience and skill in carrying the University through the turbulent years of student demonstrations that swept our country during his term of office. The historic commitment of this University to responsible and free student expression was fully vindicated under his leadership. Thousands of students gathered, spoke their minds, but did not react with any form of violence. His abiding interest in students was always evident because he continued to teach while serving as Chancellor.

He led the University through the crisis of the Speaker Ban issue, a time when proper institutional dignity was maintained while the debate raged. Dr. Sitterson petitioned for, obtained, and announced The William R. Kenan, Jr. Professorships made possible by a $5 million grant to the University at Chapel Hill by The William R. Kenan, Jr. Charitable Trust. This was the capstone event of his efforts at enhancing faculty strength and quality.

This good and noble spirit continues his active involvement with the University, and on most days, along about one o'clock in the afternoon, you will find him and Bill Aycock on the first tee at Finley Golf Course.

Chancellor Carlyle Sitterson

Ferebee Taylor came back to Chapel Hill after a successful career in the law in New York. I invited him to join me as a Vice-President of the University, and he gave his full strength and power to the task. He was a principal force in the development of state policy for restructuring publicly-funded institutions in North Carolina, and he played a major role in the emergence of the system we have today.

Among all the events and achievements of his service as Chancellor, I am sure he would point to the enormous success of his planning for library expansions and development as his most important undertaking. Shepherding carefully the sale of the University utility systems to realize the necessary dollars, Ferebee Taylor brought about the most comprehensive advances in library resources and facilities of any major university in the land. A similar effort led by him extended greater health care to citizens of the state.

He became a teacher of the law again following his years as Chancellor, and he conducts for his students lively classes and stimulating seminars on major legal issues.

Chancellor Ferebee Taylor

Presently, Christopher Fordham occupies the Chancellor's chair, having come to the position after a most successful tenure as Dean of the School of Medicine and head of Health Sciences. As Chancellor, he has extended the Area Health Education Centers across the state to bring medical assistance to all of our citizens while at the same time providing major training opportunities for students in the health sciences.

Thus far in his administration, I would point to the successful work he has done in organizing the development activities of the University and relating those major efforts to the approaching Bicentennial celebration. Deserving of special recognition and citation are his efforts to revitalize the relationships of the University with the public schools of the state. The Lyndhurst Program, the math-science network, and many other related activities clearly manifest his personal commitment to lead in this effort and place the power of the institution into the common cause of improving and extending educational opportunities to all the young people of the state.

These all too inadequate references do not reflect the hundreds of hours these men spent simply serving the University in the day-by-day work of speaking, presiding, traveling, listening, mediating, inspiring, and serving all of us. Being so visible, their every action was subject to judgment and criticism—often unfairly and unjustly made. They experienced the loneliness decision-makers know and the absence from family and home at night and on weekends. Like all leaders, they experienced weariness, fatigue and pain.

But the important circumstance is that they persevered, they achieved, and they led the University to greater levels of excellence and a more splendid posture in the world community of learning. To each of these noble spirits our debt is great; that each of them lives and moves among us today brings us great joy.

Chancellor Christopher Fordham

A moment of joy is shared by (left to right) President Frank Porter Graham, Chancellor Robert House, Chancellor Carlyle Sitterson, President William Friday, President Gordon Gray, and Governor Dan K. Moore.

WILLIAM C. FRIDAY, A GREAT AND DISTINGUISHED PRESIDENT

by Charles Kuralt

Only two Presidents have ever meant anything to me, and I assumed both of them would be President forever. President Roosevelt was the first one. He was President when I was born, and in all the years of my early youth, he was the President. It was not possible for me to imagine that anybody else ever had been President or would ever be President after Roosevelt. Everything he did was right, as far as Onslow County was concerned. He brought electric light to the farms and put the boys to work on the CCC and fought the Germans and the Japanese. He did all these things *personally*. He was the *President*.

The other President to whom I have felt completely devoted is President Friday. He entered my life, the lives of most of us, not very long after the other President died. He is the President of the thing we have loved almost as much as our country—our University. And it is impossible for some of us to remember anybody before him except Frank Graham, of course, or to imagine anybody after him. He took one of the better state universities of the South, a good provincial school, and transformed it into one of the great universities of the nation. The school that once served the state now serves the world—while serving the *state* in ways unimagined by anybody but Bill Friday when Bill Friday became its president. The University when he arrived was a village of scholars on a hill, with branches for farmers and mill hands at Raleigh, and for women, whose place in education was considered a shade inferior to that of farmers and mill hands, at Greensboro. The University when he leaves this year will be 16 schools with strengths of their own, from Wilmington, Elizabeth City and Pembroke, to Asheville, Boone and Cullowhee. And as far as I have been able to tell, Bill Friday did all this *personally,* without any help from anybody, except maybe some from Ida, the way Roosevelt was sometimes helped by Eleanor.

He was born in Virginia, through no fault of his own, and grew up in Dallas, North Carolina. If you don't know where Dallas is, it is about halfway between Stanley and Ranlo. I, who started out writing high school sports for the *Charlotte News,* am impressed that he started out writing sports for the *Gastonia Gazette.* Now, Charlotte was the metropolis of the Carolinas, and the *Charlotte News* a widely circulated newspaper. Gastonia, on the other hand, is best remembered by Carl Sandburg's remark: "That town sounds like a stomach disease." And the *Gastonia Gazette* was a paper that never circulated farther than Dallas, Stanley and Ranlo. How it was, therefore, that he went on to become the President of the University, and I went on to make a living covering musical saw players, and swimming pigs, and guys who have cars that run on corncobs, must be explained by other factors.

His undergraduate degree was in textile engineering from State—State College, that is, not North Carolina State University or the University of North Carolina at Raleigh, the faintly ridiculous title by which the old cow college now styles itself.

After helping to win President Roosevelt's war, President Friday came to his true home at last. . . Chapel Hill, where he won his law degree in 1948.

Frank Graham made him Assistant Dean of Students. When I came along, he was assistant to President Gordon Gray and Secretary of the University. I was a reporter for the *Daily Tar Heel* covering South Building. Gordon Gray was far too busy to talk to the student press. Chancellor House did not feel he had been placed in office to waste his time answering impertinent questions from the *Daily Tar Heel*. . . and in fact there was only one knowledgeable person in the administration who felt the *Daily Tar Heel* had better be talked to, from time to time, and that is how Bill Friday became my Deep Throat within the University Administration. I wrote a lot of stories which began, "South Building sources say. . ." Bill Friday was the South Building sources, all of them. He made South Building seem to make sense, and warded off many a potential controversy, because his patient explanations of things made such good sense. He was a patient explainer, a moderator, a calm advocate, which he has continued to be all these years, to the great good fortune of the University and the state.

He has been involved in much controversy, as any president of a volatile institution in a growing state would have been. It helped that he was right about everything. He was right about the Dixie Classic, which he shut down when criminals took a hand in it. He was right about the Speaker Ban law which threatened to destroy academic freedom and thus destroy the University; and Bill Friday's determined and successful opposition to that iniquitous and unconstitutional law was his finest hour at Chapel Hill. He saw what the Research Triangle was going to become before anybody else saw it. He saw what the University at Chapel Hill could be when most everybody else in the state was satisfied with what it already was. He has been a great president of the University of North Carolina. His latest honor is the Distinguished Service Award for Lifetime Achievement of the American Council on Education, an award given only eight times previously, to the likes of Father Hesburgh, Clark Kerr and David Riesman. And he has had many other honors.

As to who will replace him in the office on Raleigh Road, I have already said I can't imagine. The truth is—as one of the members of the search committee sighed and remarked to me—Bill Friday is irreplaceable.

Hugh Morton

After 30 years as the University's President, William Clyde Friday (back to camera) leaves the limelight as C.D. Spangler (center of photo) is named his successor at this meeting of the Board of Governors.

WE BELIEVED IN EACH OTHER

by Charlie "Choo Choo" Justice

Other than the night Sarah agreed to marry me, the greatest honors in my life came the two times I finished runner-up in the voting for the Heisman Trophy. The reason I felt so honored was because I knew it made my teammates feel good about the job they had done. No back—not Staubach or Dorsett or Walker (Doak or Herschel)—ever won the Heisman by himself. It takes great coaching, great teamwork, great blocking and—because footballs sometimes bounce funny—a whole lot of luck.

Every chance I get I like to brag about my Carolina teammates. I naturally think first about the biggest kidder I ever played with, Chan Highsmith, a truly great center and tackle who broke his back and missed our Sugar Bowl game in 1946. A wonderful friend, Chan died of a heart attack at 35.

Ted Hazlewood was an outstanding, 6'3" lineman who could run like a deer. Ted later coached at UNC under Carl Snavely and then played with me on the Redskins.

Ralph Strayhorn was our 1946 captain. With all the so-called "specialists" playing today, we've almost forgotten that some fellows used to play the *entire* game—on offense *and* defense. That's what Ralph did, and there was none finer.

Sid Varney, Bob Mitten and Dan Stigman were three Pennsylvania players who spent their Saturday afternoons making me look a lot better than I really was. Sid, now a college vice president, was known as "the Toy Bulldog," and he was as tough as whit leather. Bob, who was humble, quiet and just as rugged as Sid, died in his early forties. It was Dan who made the block that beat Georgia in 1948. I was about to get creamed when he came out of nowhere to make that big block; he left me 85 yards of open field to the goal line.

Everyone knows about my great friend, Art Weiner, the All-American end who was dreaded by every linebacker we faced. It's interesting that we had a second-string end backing up Art (John Tandy) who might have made All-American himself if Art had enrolled elsewhere.

All of my teammates did well after we left Carolina, and many of them have been successful teachers, coaches, lawyers, military officers and businessmen. Dr. Bill Thornton of course, has been an astronaut and a great American hero. Bob "Fuzzy" Cox of Chapel Hill has certainly represented us well; he was elected National President of the Jaycees. Ernie Williamson *was* the Rams Club for many years. Jim Camp is a leading executive at the Research Triangle Institute. All-American Kenny Powell, "Big Bill" Smith, Mike Rubish, Paul Rizzo, Joe Neikirk, Johnny Clements—they've all been leaders in their communities.

People have asked me how it's possible that the members of those teams and our wives still have reunions every year. It's because we were a *team,* a family, and it was no big deal to us whether Art or Kenny or I or somebody else got the publicity. We loved and cared for each other then, and we still do today. Whatever the assignment was, together we knew we could do it, even when some of us were injured. That's what won so many games for us: We believed in each other.

Hugh Morton

With great blocking like this, it's easy to see why "Choo Choo" gave all the credit for his success to his teammates.

Hugh Morton

Unable to play because of injuries, a dejected Charlie Justice couldn't bear to watch the 'Heels lose to Notre Dame in Yankee Stadium.

40 YEARS OF CAROLINA FOOTBALL MEMORIES

by Neale Patrick

When I covered my very first Carolina football game as a professional sportswriter 40 years ago, in my wildest dreams I could not have imagined that some 300 home and away games later I would be called on to sit down and sift through a literal *mountain* of faded clippings and old, crinkled columns. The process was worth it, though, because of the memories, the roars, the late-night deadlines, and the pleasant trips it brought back. Remember with me. . .

Do you recall the day in 1948 when Texas' football Longhorns faced roundup time in Kenan Stadium? Were you there on a Thanksgiving afternoon in 1959 when North Carolina played at arch-rival Duke? And did you know that the final point-after-touchdown attempts in both games played an ironic role in the final scores?

Texas and Duke were the victims of super-charged Tar Heel teams in two of the finest performances and most memorable games in the past 40 years of Carolina football. An errant placement in one game and a two-point conversion in the other etched the scores forever in the memory of Carolina fans.

The Longhorns had humiliated Carolina, 34-0, in Texas the previous year. The Tar Heels sought revenge and struck quickly. Charlie Justice ran back a punt 37 yards and two plays later he hit Art Weiner with a 20-yard touchdown pass. Justice scored himself and passed to Bob Cox for another TD, all in the first 12 minutes. True-toed Cox uncharacteristically missed the extra point after Carolina's fifth touchdown. Ironically, those 34 points duplicated Texas' total the year before: UNC 34, a shocked Texas 7. Sweet revenge!

Carolina was near-perfect in the 1959 battle at Duke, a game dedicated to Coach Jim Tatum, who died several months earlier. Tatum had envisioned the Tar Heels as a national power that season, but they went into the final game with a 4-5 record.

Carolina swept to a 28-0 halftime lead and opened the second half with one of the magic moments of Tar Heel football history. Don Kolchak, a six-two, 230-pound, tackle-sized fullback, returned the kickoff 93 yards for a touchdown. The Tar Heels continued to do everything right, scoring two more touchdowns for a 48-0 lead in the fourth quarter.

Bob Shupin had methodically kicked the extra points following the first six touchdowns, but the Tar Heels themselves envisioned a score for the ages. Reserve quarterback Ray Farris ran a two-point conversion and engraved the most unforgettable score in Carolina football history: 50-0.

Countless other memories are associated with Carolina blue ribbons of football—memorable games, thrilling individual performances and outstanding plays. Skipping over the chalklines of history:

That most vivid football memory of all: Senior Kelvin Bryant scored a record-breaking *sixth* touchdown against East Carolina in 1981. Without pomp or fanfare Bryant jogged through the end zone and presented the ball to his superstar teammate, Steve Streater, who was confined to a wheelchair by a tragic automobile accident earlier that year.

Carolina was host to Duke in a football "first" in 1983, the first game under the (portable) lights at Kenan Stadium. Duke quarterback Ben Bennett set an NCAA passing record that night but Carolina was not to be denied in the historical game. Tyrone Anthony tied the score with a 54-yard run in the fourth quarter and Scott Stankavage scored with two minutes to play to clinch a 34-27 victory.

High-scoring Carolina-Duke games are traditional in recent years. Don McCauley's greatest performance in 1970 was one to remember. He ran for a then-school record of 279 yards and five touchdowns in 47 carries, leading a 59-34 victory. The figures highlighted McCauley's season rushing total of 1,720 yards, then an NCAA record and still tops in the UNC record book.

Mike Voight, another in the long list of Carolina's great running backs, nearly duplicated McCauley's feat in 1976. He also carried the ball 47 times, gained 261 yards and scored a two-point conversion in the final seconds to beat the Blue Devils, 39-38. Voight gained 1,407 yards that season, second-high total for a Tar Heel.

All American Art Weiner, a freight train in the open field.

Two other outstanding Carolina running backs teamed-up on Duke in 1980. Kelvin Bryant gained 199 yards and "Famous Amos" Lawrence 143 in a 44-21 win. Both surpassed the 1,000-yard rushing figure for the season in that game.

It takes only a short memory to focus on the game at Duke in 1986. Carolina scored all five touchdowns on plays ranging from 32 to 82 yards, plus a 50-yard field goal. Eric Starr scored on dashes of 62 and 57 yards and Mark Maye fired touchdown passes of 82 and 51 yards, the latter to Eric Lewis with less than three minutes to play in a 42-35 win.

The Tar Heels recorded their first post-season win in the 1963 Gator Bowl, grounding the Air Force Academy, 35-0. Ken Willard scored the first touchdown, gained 94 yards and was named the MVP of the game.

The Gator Bowl of 1981 is remembered for things unseen, rather than seen. A dense fog "blacked-out" the action for the fans, while sportswriters and the public address announcer followed the game on the pressbox television monitors (ground-level cameras). Kelvin Bryant (148 yards) and Ethan Horton (144 yards) provided a 31-10 lead midway in the fourth quarter, and the Tar Heels had to hold on to defeat Arkansas, 34-27.

Great individual plays often overshadow the game itself, such as the brilliance of two Justice runs, a 74-yard masterpiece of open field running against Tennessee in 1946 and his 43-yard weaving and dodging against Duke in 1948.

Few field goals are as well-remembered as the long one Max "Bee" Chapman kicked in the final seconds to beat Duke 16-14 in 1963, clinching the Tar Heels' first Gator Bowl bid.

Three Carolina ends have added defensive gems to Carolina treasured memories. Lawrence Taylor sacked Clemson's quarterback to kill a Tiger threat in the final moments of a 24-19 win in 1980. Art Weiner, noted for his pass-catching feats, blocked a Mike Souchak field goal with only seconds remaining, saving Carolina's 21-20 win at Duke in 1949. Mike Greenday ran back a pass interception 43 yards for the touchdown which clinched Carolina's only victory over Notre Dame, 12-7, in 1960.

Bob Gantt, a fire-plug-sized halfback with the nickname of "Goo Goo," made Carolina history with an interception against William and Mary in 1950. He pilfered the pass on his own goal line and returned it 100 yards for the longest run in the Tar Heel record books.

Each of us cherishes different memories from autumn Saturdays past. I think of close friendships with men named Fetzer, Erickson, Williamson, Swofford, Cobey, Snavely, Barclay, Tatum, Hickey, Rice, Dooley and Crum. And "The Mouth of the South," Bill Currie, Jake Wade, Bob Quincy, Jack Williams, Woody Durham, and Rick Brewer. You may remember a special date you had; or a party afterwards; or the new suit you wore. I remember typewriter keys that broke and tires that went flat on the way home to Gastonia. But mostly I recall the crisp air, the blue sky, the clang of the cheerleaders' victory bell, and the roar—always the roar.

When they were younger, Steve Streater and Lawrence Taylor. . . hung out in the student union game room, taking on the world in eight ball. They fished for bream at Dr. Bigger's pond on the edge of Chapel Hill. They played a mean game of cards.

For three years they were inseparable. Roommates with the same dream. Until April 30, 1981. Streater, a defensive back, had just signed a free-agent contract with the Washington Redskins. Driving home from the airport in the rain that same night, he lost control of his new sports car on a slippery road, and the crash left him paralyzed from the chest down.

Taylor, the Number 1 draft choice of the New York Giants, was attending rookie minicamp when he heard about the accident. Within hours he was at Streater's bedside. "I looked up and saw the fear in Lawrence's face," Streater recalls. "He began beating on the walls, beating on the door, and he screamed, 'Steve, get up from there! This isn't you! Steve, you *must* get up!'"

Taylor was crying uncontrollably. "Have you ever seen a 6'4," 240-pound man fall apart?" Streater asks. "Lawrence Taylor, so strong, so invincible. He could do anything. He'd soar 10 feet in the air to block punts, leap over piles, tackle three people at once. For the first time I told Lawrence I loved him. He stopped crying, and he told me I'd pull through, that with his help, someday I'd walk again."

Later, Taylor broke down again, this time in the arms of his fiancée, Linda Cooley. "Why couldn't I have been driving?" he cried. "Why couldn't it have been me in that car instead?" That night Lawrence told Linda he wanted to quit football. . . .

Six years later Lawrence Taylor was the first defensive player in NFL history to be the consensus Most Valuable Player. . . .

Jill Lieber
Sports Illustrated

Kelvin Bryant (left) presents his touchdown pigskin to a jubilant Steve Streater.

Before he became America's most popular sheriff, Andy Griffith of Mount Airy entertained a delighted Kenan Stadium audience with his greatest-of-all-talking-records, "What It Was Was Football."

"WHAT IT WAS WAS FOOTBALL"

by Andy Griffith

It was back last October, I believe it was. We was going to hold a tent service off at this college town, and we got there about dinner time on Saturday. Different ones of us thought that we ought to get us a mouthful to eat before that we set up the tent. So we got off of the truck and followed this little bunch of people through this small, little bitty patch of woods there, and we come up on a big sign that says, "Get something to eat here." I went up and got me two hot dogs and a big orange drink, and before I could take a mouthful of that food, this whole raft of people come up around me and got me to where I couldn't eat nothing, up-like, and I dropped my big orange drink. Well, friends, they commenced to move, and there wasn't so much that I could do but move with 'em.

Well, we commenced to go through all kinds of doors and gates and I don't know what-all, and I looked up over one of 'em and it says, "North Gate." We kept on a-goin' through there, and pretty soon we come up on a young boy, and he says, "Ticket, please." And I says, "Friend, I don't have a ticket; I don't even know where it is that I'm a-goin'!" Well, he says, "Come out as quick as you can." And I says, "I'll do 'er; I'll turn right around the first chance I get."

Well, we kept on a-movin' through there, and pretty soon everybody got where it was that they was a-goin', because they parted and I could see pretty good. And what I seen was this whole raft of people a-sittin' on these two banks and a-lookin' at one another across this pretty little green cow pasture.

Somebody had took and drawed white lines all over it and drove posts in it, and I don't know what-all, and I looked down there and I seen five or six convicts *a-runnin' up and down and a-blowin' whistles. And then I looked down there and I seen these pretty girls wearin' these little bitty short dresses and a-dancin' around, and so I thought I'd sit down and see what it was that was a-goin' to happen.*

About the time I got set-down good I looked down there and I seen thirty or forty men come runnin' out of one end of a great, big outhouse *down there, and everybody where I was a-settin' got up and* hollered! *And about that time thirty or forty come runnin' out of the* other *end of that outhouse, and the other bankfull,* they *got up and hollered! And I asked this fella that was sittin' beside of me, "Friend, what is it that they're a-hollerin' for?" Well, he* whopped *me on the back and he says, "Buddy,* have a drink!" *I says, "Well, I believe I will have another big orange."* I got it and set back down.

When I got there again I seen that them men had got in two little bitty bunches down there, real close together, and they voted. *They elected one man apiece, and them two men come out in the middle of that cow pasture and shook hands like they hadn't seen one another in a long time. Then a convict come over to where they was a-standin', and he took out a quarter and they commenced to odd-man* right there! *After awhile I seen what it was that they was odd-mannin' for. It was that both bunchesfull of them men wanted this funny lookin' little pumpkin to play with. And I know, friends, that they couldn't eat it because they kicked it the whole evenin' and it never busted!*

Both bunchesfull wanted that thing. One bunch got it and it made the other bunch just as mad *as they could be! Friends, I seen that evenin' the awfulest fight that I have ever* seen *in my* life!!! *They would* run *at one-another and* kick *one-another and* throw one-another down *and* stomp on one-another *and* griiiiind (!!) *their feet in one another, and I don't know* what-all, *and just as fast as one of 'em would get hurt, they'd tote him off and* run another one on!!!

Well, they done that as long as I set there, but pretty soon this boy that had said, "Ticket, please," he come up to me and he says, "Friend, you're gonna have to leave because it is that you don't have a ticket." And I says, "Well, allright." And I got up and left.

I don't know, friends, to this day what it was that they was a-doin' down there, but I have studied about it. I think that it's some kindly of a contest where they see which bunchfull of them men can take that pumpkin and run from one end of that cow pasture to the other without either gettin' knocked down or steppin' in somethin'.

Chip Henderson

Fan fanaticism is the right of youngsters as well as adults, so long as your heart is in the right place and your color is Carolina blue.

Chip Henderson

With interest and admiration a tiny Tar Heel watches the brawny antics of the big guys.

Chip Henderson

"So it's Rah! Rah! Care-lina-lina..."

Chip Henderson

Above the approving shouts and cheers from the bleachers, the University band blares out a musical salute. Band director John F. Yesulaitis, fondly known as Major Y, has completed 23 seasons as Tar Heel Tooter Tutor.

Chip Henderson

Rameses strikes a threatening pose before the foes of UNC. His symbolic first ancestor was Rameses I of Texas, born in the 1920's.

Chip Henderson

Harris Barton (no. 67) was the first round draft pick of the San Francisco 49ers in 1987.

Chip Henderson

The Georgia Tech Yellow Jacket has few friends in Kenan.

Chip Henderson

UNC Head Coach Dick Crum has ears and eyes for the game. Through nine seasons his teams had compiled a record of 67 wins, 35 losses and 3 ties.

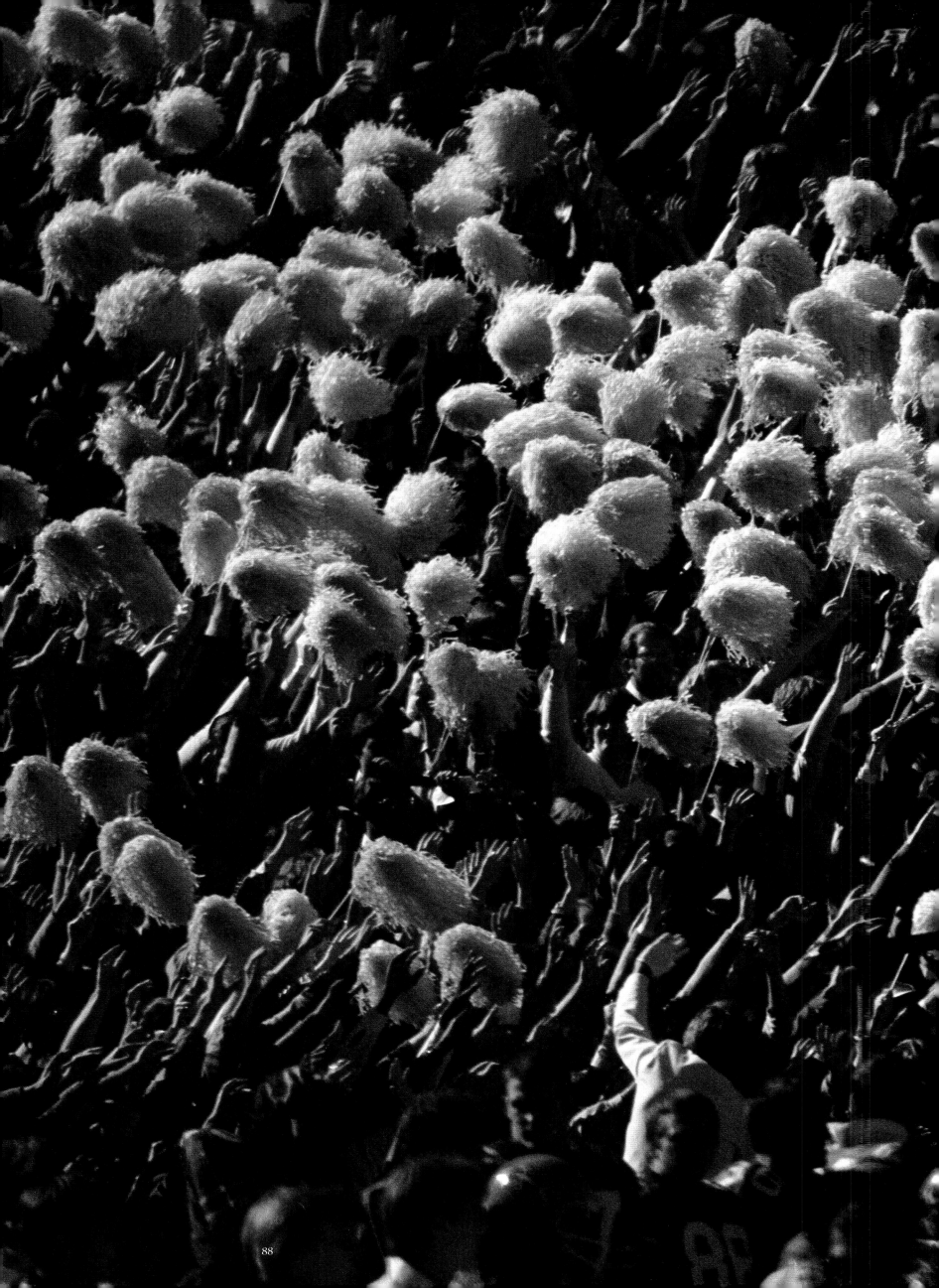

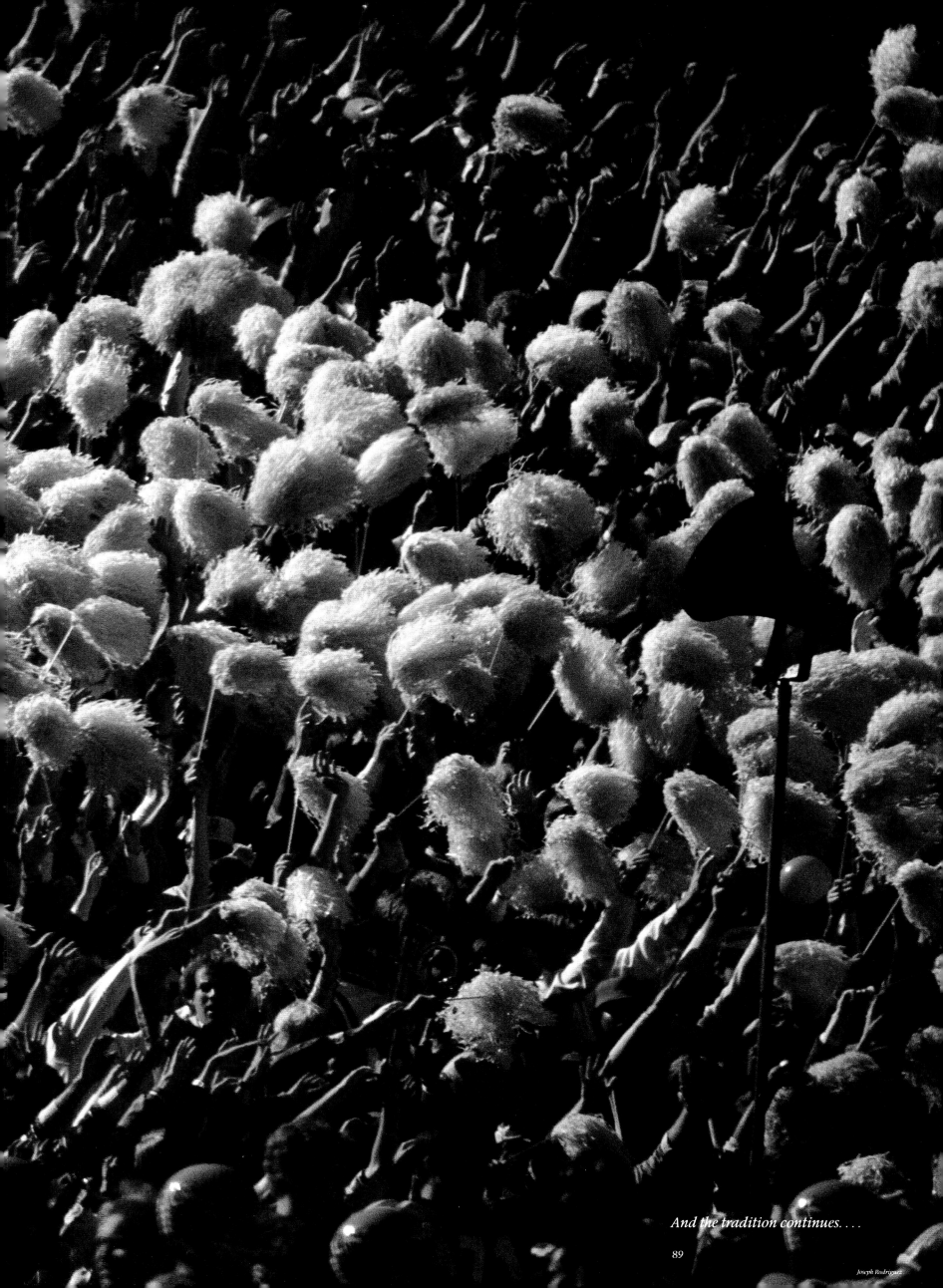

And the tradition continues. . . .

Joseph Rodriguez

UNC Photo Lab

Many students agreed that Dr. James Penrose Harland was the University's most influential professor during the 1940's and 1950's.

MEMOIR OF A HAPPY CLASSROOM

by C.D. Spangler, Jr.

Some young people have the unfortunate idea that learning is a painful exercise. From the 1920's to the 1960's, legions of students were relieved of that notion by a remarkable Chapel Hill professor, James Penrose Harland. I studied under Dr. Harland in 1953, and his was one of the happiest classrooms I ever encountered.

Dr. Harland taught archaeology. This was not a subject that teenagers naturally gravitated to in the early 'fifties—or maybe ever—but Dr. Harland's courses were among the most popular on campus. Looking back, I believe there were two reasons for this. First of all, the students just liked Dr. Harland. He was relentlessly cheerful, a legendary wit, and he managed to convey the idea that he genuinely liked *us.*

The second reason students flocked to his classes was that Dr. Harland seemed constitutionally unable to give a grade lower than an A. Now that was a powerful attraction.

I didn't object to getting an A, but the main reason I signed up for archaeology was to find out why all my friends talked about Dr. Harland. I barely knew what archaeology was when I found myself sitting there in his classroom with more than a hundred other students, in a course that would open my eyes to the wonders of ancient Greece.

Dr. Harland, known as "Chick" to the faculty and as "Mr. Chips" to many of us, was born in New Jersey and graduated from Princeton in 1909 with a Phi Beta Kappa key and a degree in archaeology and classics. He combined this with a brilliant record in track: I am told he once tied the world record at a 60-yard event at Madison Square Garden. After graduation, he went off to Greece, where he studied at the American School of Classical Studies at Athens before returning to Princeton for his master's and doctoral degrees.

By 1927, Dr. Harland had found a permanent home on the faculty at Chapel Hill, where he taught for 36 years. In an interview once, he said he had more than 1,000 students in a single year. He did not say he knew them all by name, yet I am certain he did. He took part in practically everything on campus, remaining a sports fan and participating with gusto in faculty-student competitions.

He earned a reputation as a practical joker. One of his victims was Katherine Carmichael, the dean of women. Once, before she embarked on a voyage to the Philippines, Dr. Harland wrote to the ship's captain that she was an expert trombonist, but too shy to admit it. On her return, Dean Carmichael regaled the faculty with stories of her frantic attempts to convince the ship's concert master that, in fact, she had never held a trombone to her lips. Not all Dr. Harland's potential victims were as gullible as the ship's captain. He used to tell a yarn about the time he pretended to be the King of Greece. He was in Livadia, in Central Greece, when he decided to pull this stunt. Speaking in fluent Greek, he identified himself as King to a young woman on the street, and said that he had got lost while looking for the local palace. Not duped, she courteously gave him directions. Following her instructions, he ended up at a public men's room.

Stories of Dr. Harland's wit and sense of humor abound in Chapel Hill. After his wife pleaded with him to rake leaves before a large party they were giving, he demurred, but erected a sign for the guests with the message: "These leaves tastefully arranged by nature."

Dr. Harland brought this merry spirit into the classroom; his lectures were as entertaining as they were erudite. We would sit there in a darkened theater, watching slides —many taken by the professor himself—of ruins, of digs, of ancient pots and statues. We got a healthy dose of mythology and Old Testament history along the way. Some students, short on sleep from adventures of the previous night, would doze off in class. As far as I could tell, that never bothered Dr. Harland, who taught for the sheer joy of teaching and, I feel certain, for the chance that he could awaken some of us to the magic of ancient history and far-away places.

In my case, and I suspect I am typical, he succeeded. As an adult, I have had the good fortune to make four visits to Greece. I have been to Mycenae, visited the ruins at Knossos on Crete, lingered on the Acropolis, and spent countless hours in museums. Dr. Harland's course helped lure me there, and kept me going back. Often, walking through some site or standing before a museum artifact, one of Dr. Harland's slides would creep into my mind, and fragments remembered from one of his lectures would help me understand what I was seeing. Once at Delphi, home of the oracle, I disobeyed the guides and inserted my foot into an opening in the ground from which, as I recall the story, the oracle used to speak. Something happened, and before I knew it, I had sprained my ankle. Limping around Greece for the rest of the trip, I enjoyed reflecting on what Dr. Harland could have made of that story!

When I told one of my colleagues I wanted to write a memoir about Dr. Harland for this book, the response was unenthusiastic. Wasn't I afraid of sending a message to the 7,400 members of the faculty throughout the University of North Carolina that I was in favor of crip courses? Well then, for the record: I am not an advocate of crip courses. But I am in favor of professors like James Penrose Harland. So how, I was asked, do I deal with the undeniable fact that Dr. Harland's grading system—an A to virtually everybody—made his courses the very archetype of crip?

My answer is that life is complex. While I believe that many great rewards come only with hard work, I also believe that a professor's mission is to evoke from his or her students a lifelong love of learning, and that Dr. Harland was a master at it. As a businessman, it sometimes occurred to me that Dr. Harland also knew a thing or two about marketing. A course like archaeology may be difficult to sell without some extra come-on. That he could pack in a thousand students a year, and make his course so memorable to so many of us, is all the proof of his proficiency I need.

Anthony F. Jenzano with his student/astronaut trainee Captain Alan B. Shepard, who became the first American in space.

PREPARING FOR THE SPACE AGE

by William E. Thornton, M.D.

So what do you take from UNC on your first 99 trips around the world in Challenger? There was an optical instrument from the Physics Department; and there were some ceremonial items, all carefully approved and stowed by NASA. More importantly, though, were unseen lessons learned at the University in the 1950's—lessons which made it possible to take the trip.

The body carried some minor gridiron scars from four years of being a "meatball" against the likes of Weiner, Holdash and Justice. Anything physical in the Astronaut Program was easy after facing those gentlemen. In fact, the Space Shuttle treadmill probably had its origin in those post-scrimmage wind sprints overseen by that master of all things, football Coach Carl Snavely.

Packed in lockers on that first flight was a small medical laboratory with electro-physiological devices to study Space Motion Sickness, an illness unlike anything ever seen on Earth. A solid, basic education in math, physics and medicine was essential to design and build such instruments, and Drs. Shearin, Fussel, Whyburn and too many others to name, made sure we got that. But the University provided something more, something greater—a tolerance and a view for the future as well as an abiding respect for the already proven. Dr. Ev Palmatier aided and encouraged, as much by example as anything else, this totally out-classed student to complete a course that was dominated by brilliant physics students. Later, he also contributed directly to the development of several important instruments for space travel. Dr. Masket also helped, and one of his graduate students, John Lindsay, was then preparing for the day when he would be instrumental in the launching of the first large NASA scientific satellites.

Not all of the teaching at the University came in classrooms and labs. My undergraduate participation in the Air Force ROTC program led to three years of military service, and by the end of that training I had developed the unheard-of notion that electronics and instrumentation could be useful in medicine. Only two medical complexes in the country would consider exploring such experiments—Mass General and the then-new medical school and hospital at UNC.

In 1955 a collaboration began with Dr. Dave Davis, and that teaming together ultimately resulted in my enrolling at UNC Medical School and, later, in Memorial Hospital's being equipped with many one-of-a-kind instruments, including operating and recovery rooms monitored by radio telemetry, extended monitoring of heart patients with tape recordings, and the first continuously computer-analyzed EKG studies. Two years before Alan

Shepard's EKG was sent back from space, we were routinely using telemetry for EKG, EEG, EMG and many other signals. Much of the medical apparatus that I took with me, or sent into space on later missions, had its genesis in Phillips Hall and Memorial Hospital.

As important as being able to make tools is to know what needs investigation, and how to make such investigations. In 1959 the medical school's primary goal was to train good physicians to take care of patients across the state, and that they did very well. Dr. Newt Fischer and many others taught medicine such that students never had to worry about their skills. The enlightenment of the greater University extended to the med school, where many teachers implemented a long and broad view that encouraged students to think and explore on their own. Such mental exploration is essential to physical exploration in the laboratories of Earth and space.

There were many such teachers in the medical school, including Warner Wells, Tim Thomas, and Earl Peacock in surgery, but most unforgettable was Price Heusner, who at that time was a professor of neuro-anatomy. While many of the minute details of neuro-anatomy may have been forgotten over time, when a basic understanding of it was needed to probe the human brain in space, Heusner's teaching beyond the books was there. It was almost uncanny how correct his teachings proved to be.

Long before Shuttle began to fly, the University was teaching astronauts to navigate at 18,000 MPH and faster, around the Earth and to the Moon and back, by teaching the stars and heavens. The classroom was that great gift, the Morehead Planetarium, which has demonstrated the wonders of the Universe to countless school children and provided inspiration, education and entertainment to at least one astronaut-to-be and his bride-to-be. Generations of astronauts—Lovell, Borman, Armstrong, Aldrin, Collins, et al.—were rigorously taught in Chapel Hill with the precision that only a few American planetariums could provide. Each and every one of us also remembers the after-hours socials at the home of our great professor, Tony Jenzano.

Symbols and artifacts from two space flights are now in their cases at the University. Challengers's 200 flawless orbits of Earth are a bitter-sweet memory for me. Thanks to what we learned, Space Motion Sickness is now just a nuisance, and no longer a dreaded disease. The University is still preparing its students for the Space Age, of which we have seen only the first tottering steps. It is training students in the sciences, medicine, literature—in all the disciplines—for people of all walks of life will be affected in the future by this technology which allows man to truly leave his natural home. While only a few may make the actual trip, the journey of the mind and spirit will be just as fantastic for many more on Earth.

Even in the midst of the thrill of riding the greatest of man's machines, or carving outposts in the foreign soil of the Moon or Mars, undoubtedly many will wonder at the special place of the Earth in the Universe. And some will recall, as I did, another special place—with its books and great oaks and the sound of tower bells on fall evenings when things were young and new—and be proud that they knew that place.

UNC Photo Lab

Anthony F. Jenzano, Director of the Morehead Planetarium, trained many U.S. astronauts. Shown here are (Row 1) Dr. Joseph Kerwin, Edgar Mitchell; (Row 2) Ray Zedekar, NASA official, Bruce McCandless, Jack R. Lousma, Gerald P. Carr; (Row 3) William R. Pogue, Ronald E. Evans, James B. Irwin, Thomas K. Mattingly, Don L. Lind, Dr. F. Curtis Michel; (Row 4) Vance Brand, Alfred M. Worden, Joe H. Engle, Charles M. Duke, Stuart A. Roosa, Paul J. Weitz; (Row 5) Edward G. Givens, John L. Swigert, Milton Reim, NASA official.

The sophisticated Zeiss Planetarium—it's capable of capturing the voyage of "Challenger."

Although the most valued features of Morehead Planetarium are housed indoors, the building and grounds elegantly enhance the appearance of this stretch along Franklin Street.

Hugh Morton

SCARIEST NIGHT OF MY LIFE

by Bob Timberlake

It was the fourth Saturday of March, 1957, and it seemed to Carolina students to be the most magnificent early spring that the Good Lord ever fashioned. Chapel Hill is always at its best in spring, but that particular year was picture-perfect: the daffodils came early and stayed late; the azaleas and dogwoods were promising to bloom by the end of the weekend; professors were postponing papers and quizzes; and students were already working on their tans. I was a sophomore, and—like everyone else in Chapel Hill and the state—I was all tied up in knots over our basketball team.

Only those of us who saw them play can fully appreciate just how great that team was—and how *too* perfect the season had been: 31 wins, 18 or 20 of which were "cliffhangers," and *no defeats*. We just knew there was no way we could beat Kansas (at Kansas) that night because we had just used up every available drop of human energy the night before in beating Michigan State (in *three* overtimes, no less). Everyone on campus agreed: "Let's cancel tonight's game and declare Carolina and Kansas co-national champions."

Too perfect. Warm weather blew in that week and away went our sweaters and coats. Chapel Hill seemed tense—reluctant to have a party of any kind that afternoon because we were too nervous about the game that night to be festive. We just waited. . . and waited.

We all talked about how tough it would be for the players and coaches to lose after going so far. We knew they had given everything they had for Carolina, and that they would be broken-hearted after the game that night. It just didn't seem fair that Kansas had that secret weapon, Wilt "the Stilt" Chamberlain, the tallest and strongest human since Goliath of Gath.

Younger readers may not be aware that back in the dark ages of 1957 there was no such thing as color television, but those of us at the Sigma Chi house did have a bulky back-and-white model. Carolina basketball on t.v. had never been heard of before, so it was a great treat to be able to watch it that night. Even though the screen was small and the picture was snowy, at least 100 of us somehow crammed into the living room to witness the event. All the windows and doors were opened; it was hot, real hot.

When we saw that Coach McGuire had chosen little (5'11") Tommy Kearns to jump center against Wilt, well, we knew for sure it was over then. Some of us crawled out the window to go get fresh air. "This can't be happening," we thought. "It's 31-0 and we're going to get creamed."

Somehow, some way, the 'Heels managed to hang tough and actually appeared to have a chance of winning until, in the 39th minute of play, our David (Lennie Rosenbluth—Mister Everything) fouled out. Out the window we dove for more fresh air, until suddenly we heard shouts of, "We scored! We scored! You guys get back in here!"

Sure enough, those who hadn't fouled out—Tommy, Joe Quigg, Pete Brennan, Bob Cunningham, Bob Young, Danny Lotz, and Ken Rosemond—had managed to tie the score. Three *excruciating* overtimes and two (thank you, Joe) Quigg foul shots later, Goliath lost the ball, time ran out, and a whole state went berserk.

If my memory serves me correctly, I recall that a group headed by Tony Schiffman, Mike Weaver, Sonny Lacey, John Black, Bob Stanton, and Brokie Lineweaver rounded up every roll of toilet paper in the house and "decorated" all the tree limbs between the Carolina Inn and Spero's Goody Shop. Every living soul in Chapel Hill converged on Franklin Street, and I remember that one or two folks accidentally spilled sky-blue paint all over the pavement. No malicious damage, understand; nothing was broken but the Kansas hearts. Jukeboxes played loudly all night long. It was Fats Domino's greatest hour.

How spooky it seemed exactly 25 years later (almost to the day) when our sons Dan and Ed, suffered through the same kind of agonizing game as Carolina students. Only the names for David and Goliath had changed (Worthy and Ewing). Everything else was the same—except, of course, they didn't have the privilege of watching it in black-and-white.

The 1957 Tar Heels: Wilt-beating Champs!!

"When we saw that Coach McGuire had chosen little, 5'11" Tommy Kearns (left) to jump center against 7'2" Wilt Chamberlain, well, we knew for sure it was over then."

FRANK MCGUIRE

by Dean E. Smith

     I don't suppose I've ever known anyone who is more loyal to his family and friends than Frank McGuire. Always gracious and kind to everyone from the teenage peanut vendor to the athletic director, Frank is a man who seems to sincerely believe that every person stands on the same level. That's a concept that many find difficult to grasp, but in Frank it seems to be natural, as if no one ever had to teach it to him.

     It is Frank's loyalty and concern for others that have made him the great success he is because, by positive means, he gets the most one can get from athletes (and staff members). He makes them all feel good about themselves. Imagine how good it made me feel in my first year as his assistant when—out of the clear blue—he called me into his office and said, "I'm going to New York on a recruiting trip for several days, so you take the practices while I'm gone. I think you're ready to do that."

     Frank was, and is, a man with remarkable instincts and he utilized this gift in motivating both players and coaches. He often used praise and understanding, sometimes constructive criticism and occasionally a short spell of "raising his voice." The majority of the time he was on target. He also knew that his players and staff members had to be given room to grow and to become themselves, and he found joy in watching us mature, even when we made mistakes. I've heard of other head coaches who have tried to force those under them into a particular mold. Not Frank.

     If they'd had a "Father of the Year" award in those days, Frank would've won it every year. His relationship with his son, Frankie, has always been very special. I remember how every schoolday morning he would drive Frankie to Durham's cerebral palsy school, and how every day during the summers he would delight in going home at lunchtime to fix Frankie's favorite meal: jelly and cream cheese sandwiches. Is it any wonder, then, that a man this loving and caring was able to bring out the best in men like Lennie Rosenbluth, Joe Quigg, Tommy Kearns, Pete Brennan and Bob Cunningham?

Lennie Rosenbluth and Coach Frank McGuire

Julius "Dr. J." Erving stated that if he were starting a professional team from scratch, J.R. Reid would be the first player he would pick.

Three decades after the McGuire era, Kenny Smith made First Team All-America. The dynamic senior was named All-ACC, and led the team in scoring with an average of 16.9 points per game. He finished the season with 768 assists, breaking Phil Ford's all-time school record.

Chip Henderson

Chip Henderson

A HEART'S A TERRIBLE THING TO WASTE

by Walter Spearman, spoken to Phi Beta Kappa, 1978

If I have a theme tonight, I'd like to call it "The Mind and the Heart." Obviously, you are the minds of the University. You have made Phi Beta Kappa. You have achieved academic distinction, and you deserve to be proud of you. Your professors deserve to be proud of you—and what they have helped you accomplish.

But tonight I want to ask you one other question: Where are your hearts?

Back in the 1960s, student hearts were all hanging out. Students were concerned with the world about them, war and peace, racial justice, the rights of labor and the welfare of the underprivileged, the plight of the poor and the desperation of the doomed. I had students who lay down in the streets of Chapel Hill, obstructing traffic and leading demonstrations to open theaters and eating places and hotels to Blacks. I had a student—an A student at that—who spent three months in an N.C. jail for seeking rights for those discriminated against.

Tom Wolfe, a brilliant writer and the founder of our so-called "new journalism," calls the 1970s the "Me Decade." Encounter groups, meditation groups, therapy sessions, Zen and yoga, primal therapy, sexual swinging, they all scream: "Let's talk about me! That's what is important. Never mind the other fellow. Let's talk about me and forget the rest of the world. What grade will I get? What graduate school will I be admitted to? What job can I get? What sex partner can I find? What kind of retirement benefits will my job bring me? Let's think about me!"

Where are we now? Last year, I read an editorial in The Daily Tar Heel, *my old alma mater,* entitled "Students seek status quo." The editorial quoted the director of the London School of Economics as saying self-confident students of the 1960s have been replaced by the fearful and defensive students of the 1970s who demand a defense of the status quo, of existing privileges. And the student writer concluded: "The student of the '70s has his hands full simply worrying about his own future. The idealism of the student of the '60s, striking out for utopia, has fallen by the wayside only to be replaced by a world of the survival of the fittest."

Several years ago, The New York Times *made a survey of college editors on eight campuses, from coast to coast, asking what students were most interested in. One editor reported, "This campus' 13,000 students want a place of security in an anxious world more than an opportunity to make the world more secure." And the UNC editor wrote, "Two-fifths of the students are preoccupied with trivia, about two-fifths of us sway back from concern to unconcern and about one-fifth are involved in something significant, something larger than ourselves."*

One advantage of teaching here for more than 40 years is that one sees so many college generations come and go, usually in like freshman lambs and out like senior lions. What do they do while they are here? Is it a four-year rest period—or coffee break—or beer blast—between high school graduation and a lifetime job? Or is it a period of growth, of maturing, of new ideas and expanding horizons, of trying our intellectual wings, of dedication, and service? Are they parasites who sap the University of its stored-up strength? Do they take away without replenishing? Or do they revitalize a University that may be growing tired and add their own new ideas to the University's accumulation of wisdom?

Students seem more concerned with grades today—and with getting into graduate school or medical school or law school—than with other people and the world outside. No one is willing to accept a C even if it is a well-deserved C for too little work or too sloppy work.

For the first time in my 43 years of teaching at Carolina, students call me up at home at night to explain why they may have to cut my class the next day or why they have not been able to finish a paper on time.

Don't mistake me. It is good to be concerned about grades. How else can you get an education? How else can you make Phi Beta Kappa? But let's not sacrifice the heart to the mind. Let's not forget concern and compassion from the 1960s. If the 1970s is really the "Me Decade," as writer Tom Wolfe says it is, let us try to temper the personal concerns for ourselves and for our future with great outreach to others. "ME! ME! ME!" can become a selfish scream if one constantly ignores the needs and aspirations of others. Let's not cry "wolf"—even Tom Wolfe—too often. We might keep the chiding Wolfe from our personal door by looking outside to see the world around us. Can we use our Phi Beta Kappa minds and our human hearts to make that a better world?

In one or two college generations, the pendulum swings—from apathy to activism, from callousness to concern, from selfishness to unselfishness, from the scheming mind to the roving heart.

To illustrate that swinging pendulum, let me take you over to two of my classes in journalism. I teach a class in book, movie and play reviewing. We read Judith Crist's movie reviews and hear her call The Sound of Music *the "sound of marshmallows." We recall the small boy who said, "This book tells me* more about penguins than I want to know." We remember George Bernard Shaw's classic remark: "A critic is a man who leaves no turn unstoned." We quote that infamous line: "An amateur quartet played Brahms last night; Brahms lost."

Then I teach a course in editorial writing, and my students write about very serious subjects: the purpose of education, registration, drop-add, students' rights to vote, the Honor System, abortions, freedom of the press, conditions in prison, capital punishment, Watergate, the nuclear bomb, ERA, and discrimination against Blacks and women.

One day, I asked my students to list five topics they were sufficiently concerned about to try to persuade others to their own convictions. Most of them busily jotted down something. But one girl—a very pretty girl—looked bewilderedly out the window. After class, she turned in a blank paper. "But Mr. Spearman," she said, "I'm just not concerned with anything. I think everything is just fine."

Remember, the "new commandment": "Thou shalt not commit—thyself"? She didn't, and she hadn't.

But I see commitment on every hand. Sometimes I even see a student committed to an academic course, to a term paper that excites him all through the night before he has to turn it in, to a new subject that gives him ideas he never had before, to a particular professor who may open up challenging new areas of study that had never interested him before.

Not all commitments are to great public causes. They may be to a superior basketball team. They may be commitments to a girl, but commitments that belie the old Playboy philosophy that girls, like any good accessory, are detachable and disposable. They may be commitments to become the best doctor or lawyer or nuclear physicist you are capable of being. They may be commitments to open your sorority or your fraternity to all individuals, regardless of race, creed or color.

Commitments come in various sizes. What is a small commitment to one person may be a large and meaningful one to another: the refusal to go along with popular stereotypes, the determination to think for yourself, the courage to be a non-conformist in the midst of conformity. The student who comes to Chapel Hill and gets a new idea, a new commitment, may puzzle his family back home—or even frighten the state—but he may well be building a progressive, enlightened future for his state.

The hippies used to say, "Do your thing," but I would add, "Have a thing to do." "Build, baby, build" was always a better slogan than "Burn, baby, burn."

Oh, there was apathy back in the 1960s—as well as dedicated commitment. And there is commitment today—as well as a tendency to "look out for Number One." Our task as "thinking students," as men and women with Phi Beta Kappa minds, is to use our minds in conjunction with our hearts to create the full man, the complete woman, the felicitous combination of mind and heart.

If this were to be a "Last Lecture," I'd like to wrap it all in a box and, like the boxes we used to send abroad for the starving, write "care" on it in large letters—CARE. Care about your academic work. You obviously do—or you wouldn't be here tonight. Care about the University that tries to nurture you. Care about your fellow students. Care about the world in which you live and the people who live in it with you, even those you have never seen. If you need a motto for tomorrow, change it from "Thou shalt not commit—thyself" to the one word: "Care."

Neither the faculty nor the administration nor your parents should ask you to avoid controversy. Rather, we should ask you and eternally encourage you to care about something—and to care enough to become involved.

Now even a Last Lecture has its last paragraph: I want to pass on to you the words of the two professors who meant the most to me back in the 1920s when I was a student, when I, too, was under 30. Their commitment shone round their heads like halos—and to me they were, and are, Chapel Hill and the University. We all need our heros, and these were mine. Let them be yours, too, or find new heros of your own.

Playwright Paul Green once said, "Life is like a tree forever growing." So may it prove to you.

And University President Frank Graham once wrote, "Where and when men are free, the way of progress is not subversion, the respect for the past is not reaction and the hope of the future is not revolution, where majority is without tyranny, the minority without fear, and all people have hope of building together a nobler America in a freer and fairer world."

When I was a student, Paul Green gave me a volume of his plays. On the flyleaf, he wrote: "To Walter Spearman, with a belief in his ultimate triumph."

My last words to you as a teacher are these: "I have a belief in your ultimate triumph." And I care. Develop and cultivate and use your mind—but don't sacrifice your heart."

THEY CALLED US 'FREEDOM FIGHTERS'

by Karen L. Parker

Yes, my son, it was back in 1963. It was right in the heyday of the civil rights movement in college. It was at the main branch of the University of North Carolina—in Chapel Hill. A beautiful campus, a nice place. You might consider going there yourself. The weather is a little nippier than California, but not too cold, not too hot.

From a journal, Jan. 12, 1964:"Today's rally was just wonderful. . . we met demonstrators from Durham at the Eastgate shopping center. . . it was raining and cold. . . rain had frozen on trees. . . a few snowflakes fluttered down. . . the road was muddy. . . .ATO fraternity stood outside and jeered at us."

Yes, it is a great school. Was then, is now. I've heard it called the "Ivy League of the South." It wasn't perfect, but as Southern colleges went back then, it was indeed the "Southern Part of Heaven."

From a journal, Jan. 15,1964: "It hurts. You'd think people in this community would understand more. This place is NOT liberal, but very much conservative. The town and the University.

I'm proud to have gone to Carolina. I was the first Black female undergrad to graduate from there. No, there weren't many Blacks there then. Literally a handful of undergrads in the class of 1965. Oh, there were plenty of rednecks around, but most of the whites seemed to sympathize with our Freedom Marches. And Carolina, of course, was in the forefront of that kind of thing.

Jan. 10, 1964: "On Dec. 21, the papers said the University planned to take action and perhaps even expel the demonstrators. I was shocked and became very bitter. I had always been proud of being at Carolina. . . but they are going to HAVE to expel me because I'm not giving up."

Oh, I went to jail a couple of times. Chapel Hill had a nice jail compared to a lot of other places—on that we Freedom Fighters all agreed. It wasn't like Selma. We got sprayed with water in Chapel Hill and Carrboro, threatened with bats. One crazy time we blocked all exits from town right after a Duke-Carolina basketball game. I remember sitting in an intersection on Franklin Street, the main drag. Now that was kind of scary.

South Building steps, May, 1970. The plight of UNC Food Service workers, the Kent State killings, and the U.S. invasion of Cambodia fueled this loud, but peaceful, student protest.

The sixties—a time when the youth of America shouted, "No!" to many of the Establishment's programs.

Jan. 10, 1964: "We heard that at the Rock Pile Cafe between here and Durham someone threw ammonia on some of the demonstrators. They were hospitalized for burns. They poured it down Quentin Baker's throat. His stomach was pumped three times."

There was a great feeling of pride during those marches. It was for "the cause." That's all that seemed to matter.

Ibid. "Sometimes you wonder why you are doing this—what's the good of it? We know that it is important, but so often it's like beating your head against the jail bars."

It wasn't so bad being Black on that campus, and I made some really great white friends during the civil rights days. The rank and file—"Carolina ladies and gentlemen"—didn't give us much trouble or notice.

April 13, 1964: "I was watching the Academy Awards in the dorm tonight and a group of girls was jeering at Sammy Davis, Jr., who was singing. It made me feel very low. Gave me the determination to fight and prove my worth—to 'show 'em.' I'm the only undergrad Negro girl on this campus. I'm not very well-liked by white girls. Later on Sidney Poitier won the best actor award. Many girls applauded. The group of jeerers was quiet. I got the greatest feeling to see a Negro come out on top for once."

Were we successful? Well, not as much as we would have liked. The important thing was the spirit, the message we got across.

April 30, 1964: "The newspapers have already said that the Chapel Hill Freedom Movement is dead. We're trying to show them it is not."

Well, now to be more accurate, most restaurants didn't desegregate until after the 1964 Civil Rights Act. They didn't like it, but Chapel Hill was pretty decent after that.

March 4, 1965: "The class ring will remind me of my great, sad, perplexing, enlightening, wild, bitter and free experiences here. . . . This is a beautiful, wonderful place, despite its faults."

That's why, my son, I have a Carolina decal on my car to this day. All told, it was a beautiful, wonderful place—despite its faults.

DRAFT DAYS

by Eric R. Calhoun

Downtown Raleigh, 1969.

They were all chuckling as we got out of the buses and shuffled into the Army induction center. The medical staff knew what to expect from this group sent from the Chapel Hill draft board, since we were nearly all Carolina students and since we nearly all carried a thick file of reasons why we were unfit for military service. In hindsight, I think the staff enjoyed it.

A busload of high school seniors from Roxboro or Henderson or Smithfield did not offer the same challenge. Those kids, scared and defenseless, were poked, prodded and bled and, at the end, were herded out the back door and into uniform. Our group was richer, better educated and, as was especially apparent as we stood naked in the weigh-in line, much whiter. Our determination to avoid the military was reduced to those thick medical files.

Objections to the Vietnam war flowed at different levels in each of us, but we were unanimous in our desire to avoid induction into the Army. I was acquainted with perhaps a dozen of the young men who shivered and shuffled with me from one test to another. A couple were active and participated in campus demonstrations against the war, but most were like me: generally apathetic towards active expressions of resistance, though full of bluster of a high moral tone when circumstances suggested that was called for. Thirty minutes of Walter Cronkite each evening kept us scared stiff and only superficially informed. We were concerned about our country's involvement in the war, but we were more concerned about our own personal non-involvement in the fighting. The conclusion reached after most long, looping, beer-induced debates was an unswerving commitment to avoid military service, even if you had to do so "for religious reasons."

Methods of dodging the draft varied. Thousands of young men simply hid or left. Neither technique was complex or difficult to accomplish, but both carried heavy social, economic, and legal baggage. A slightly less spontaneous and more socially acceptable technique was practiced by most in the busload of Carolina students—the quest for a 4-F classification and exemption from the draft for medical reasons.

You didn't have to go far in Chapel Hill to find advice on ruses designed to defeat the military's medical tests. Swallowing small balls of aluminum foil was alleged to mimic kidney stones and ulcers; vast quantities of coffee or sugar would fool the blood tests; dexedrine and other drugs raised the blood pressure. The staff at the induction center must have enjoyed deciphering the profusion of plague-like symptoms displayed by an otherwise apparently healthy group of Carolina sophisticates.

The safest medical ploy was to magnify through numbers of doctor's visits and tests any existing physical abnormalities. A meaningless smoker's cough became a debilitating wheeze, perhaps asthmatic. An old sports injury might turn suddenly crippling. Eyesight deteriorated, allergies flared, facial tics developed. In fact, it was miraculous that we could even drag ourselves off the bus, our collective condition was so grave.

Thousands of Carolina students served with distinction in the military during this period. Indeed, every other war story in this volume reveals the zealous enlistment of Tar Heel men, unified citizens back home, and universally-approved causes. But the war in Vietnam was different. While many believed in what America was doing in Southeast Asia, many did not. And millions of college boys didn't know *what* they believed except they didn't want to die young.

As passionate and bitter as the debates were, rarely did the issues affect friendships. Most everyone had friends who enlisted proudly and friends who opposed the war bitterly. A decision to enlist was treated with the same respect as a decision to become a conscientious objector or to flee to Canada.

Vietnam was America's first "television war." Our generation was the first to grow up in front of a television set and the first to be horrified—in color—by fire fights and napalm bombings and chemical warfare. Nightly, we memorized the names of war-torn villages smaller than Carrboro: My Lai, Binh, Xaun Loc, Vung Tau.

And then there was that excruciating winter night in 1970 when those of us about to graduate watched the nation's first televised draft lottery. Ping pong balls, each with a birthdate inscribed on it, were drawn from a barrel: Fate had been systematized. Those with birthdates on the first 200 ping pong balls chosen could count on being drafted in June or July; one in four drafted would then find his way to Vietnam. I can vividly recall to this day the anguished groans of my friends in the room whose birthdates were drawn early. Any joy felt by someone with a high number was tempered by the grief-stricken faces around him.

Then finally, in 1975, the TV networks recorded for us those vivid scenes of choppers rising from the roof of the American embassy in Saigon, desperate men and women dangling from the skids.

The war had ended, which meant the draft had officially ended, too. While the UNC classes of the sixties may not have been as universally fervent about the fighting as the classes of the 'teens and the forties, we were absolutely as sad about the dying. Young readers, learn from this tragedy: If one dies, too many die.

Six years a prisoner of war in Vietnam, Barry Bridger, UNC '62, is shown riding in Bladenboro's "Welcome Home, Barry" parade in 1973.

President John F. Kennedy is flanked (to his left) by Chancellor William B. Aycock and (to his right) President William C. F⁻day and Governor Terry Sanford on the occasion of his 1961 University Day speech in Kenan Stadium.

HE MOBILIZED THE AMERICAN SPIRIT

by Terry Sanford

Just a few weeks after we were elected, he as President and I as Governor, I we⁻t to see John F. Kennedy in Palm Beach, where he was putting together his cabinet and admir⁻stra-tion. I delivered to him President Bill Friday's request that he consider accepting an hor⁻rary degree from the University. "Is that Chapel Hill?" he responded. When I answered yes, he said, "Oh, Chapel Hill. . . that is a great school. I'd like that."

After all the necessary faculty and board approvals had been made, the Presi⁻lent received his degree before an estimated crowd of 30,000 in Kenan Stadium on October 12, 1961. Some 25 months after that University Day gathering he would make his tragic tri⁻ to Dallas.

Characteristically, he put his own stamp on the occasion. He asked if it would ⁻e all right if he did not wear the traditional mortar board hat for the ceremony. When I said ⁻ was okay, he—hatless—employed in his speech many of the themes that distinguished the re⁻ark-able strength of his administration.

He praised liberal education: "We still need men and women, educated in the l⁻beral tradition, willing to take the *long* look, undisturbed by the prejudices and slogans of th⁻ moment, who attempt to make an honest judgment on difficult events."

Some of his words are as relevant today as they were a generation ago: "Our task in this country is to do our best. . . and not to be swayed from our course by the faint-hearted or the unknowing or the threats of those who would make themselves our foes," and "We are destined, all of us here today, to live out most if not *all* of our lives in uncertainty and challenge and peril." It was a speech marked also by humor and by a call for courage. It was a speech that reached us all.

To understand the Kennedy phenomenon, it has to be seen in its place in time. We had come triumphantly through World War II and had been disillusioned by the emergence of a new and threatening adversary. That disillusionment was in part responsible for the scourge of McCarthyism. And while Europe was well on its way to recovery, there was the terrible uncertainty of the Korean War and, later, the Berlin Wall and the rising Cold War. We Americans had lost our adolescence.

Now this articulate young President appeared in our lives and he told us that we could fix things, repair the damage, face our foes and prevail. Prevail. Edward R. Murrow once said that Winston Churchill mobilized the English language and sent it into battle. John Kennedy mobilized the American spirit and sent it looking for a proud peace.

We believed him because he made it possible to believe in ourselves. He quickened our spirits after we had gone through a painful period of self-doubt.

It is difficult if not impossible to recall, for those who did not experience it, the raw excitement of the Kennedy years. Never mind his flaws or the fact that his programs may have been headed into major problems with Congress. His was the kind of inspiration we had nearly forgotten.

We Americans were not alone in our response to him. I saw his picture recently on the office wall of the Foreign Minister of Costa Rica. Similar pictures became in many countries a kind of American icon.

All the more devastating, then, when President Kennedy was ripped from our lives. The shock cannot be exaggerated. Our country was paralyzed with grief. Nearly all of us can remember precisely what we were doing when we heard the news. We are permanently imprinted with that moment. The effect on the world was disbelief and despair. One of the unforgettable images of the funeral was the long line of world leaders, led by the President's widow and France's President DeGaulle, who walked somberly behind the casket.

The President's death came on the eve of the annual Duke-Carolina football game. Thirty-one floats were forming for the pre-game parade in front of Woollen Gymnasium when news of the assassination became known in Chapel Hill. The parade dissolved even before the student organizers formally called it off. The game itself was postponed. Crowds of people in shock gathered on the campus and downtown. Many instructors called off classes. Church services were held as early as three hours after the announcement was made. ROTC buglers played taps at the campus flag pole. The South Building bell tolled for the President, and for all of us.

In Washington, one of the President's aides said to a companion that he would never smile again. You'll smile again, the companion answered, but you'll never be young again.

It is tempting to measure our lives in the context of apocalyptic events: before and after wars, for example. That method, of course, is an over-simplification. Our lives are played out day by day, and the courses we take are directed by small or large decisions each of us makes individually.

Nevertheless, the quickening of the spirits that John Kennedy's presidency gave us is a reminder that we are limited in our achievements only by the quality of our aspirations. It was a rare gift.

It is not unlike another gift. Those of us who have dwelled in the spirit of Frank Porter Graham's Chapel Hill have felt his inspiration ever since. We can count ourselves doubly fortunate.

ADDRESS OF U.S. PRESIDENT JOHN F. KENNEDY

OCTOBER 12, 1961—KENAN STADIUM

President Friday, Mr. Chancellor, Governor Sanford, members of the faculty, ladies and gentlemen. I am honored today to be admitted to the fellowship of this ancient and distinguished university, and I am pleased to receive in the short space of one or two minutes the honor for which you spend over four years of your lives working. But whether the degree be honorary or earned, it is a proud symbol of this university and this state.

North Carolina has long been identified with enlightened and progressive leaders and people, and I can think of no more important reason for that reputation than this university. Distinguished presidents, like Presidents Graham and Gray, distinguished leaders like Secretary of Commerce Luther Hodges, distinguished members of the Congressional delegation, carry out a tradition which stretches back to the beginning of this school, that is, that the graduate of this university is a man of his nation as well as a man of his time.

It is my hope, in a changing world when untold possibilities lie before North Carolina and indeed the entire South and country, that this university will still hew to the old line of the responsibility that its graduates owe to the community at large.

It is my hope that in your time, too, you will be willing to give to the state and country a portion of your lives and all *of your knowledge and* all *of your loyalty.*

I want to emphasize in the great concentration which we now place upon scientists and engineers, how much we still need the men and women, educated in the liberal tradition, willing to take the long *look, undisturbed by the prejudices and slogans of the moment, who attempt to make an honest judgment on difficult events. This university has a more important function today than ever before, and therefore I am proud as President of the United States and as a graduate of a small, land grant college in Massachusetts—Harvard University—to come to this center of education.*

Those of you who regard my profession of political life with some disdain should remember that it made it possible for me to move from being an obscure lieutenant in the United States Navy to Commander-in-Chief in fourteen years with very little technical competence. But more than that I hope that you will realize that from the beginning of this country, and especially in North Carolina, there has been the closest link between educated men and women and politics and government.

This is a great institution with a great tradition, and with devoted alumni, and with the support of the people of this state. Its establishment and continued functioning, like that of all great universities, has required great sacrifice by the people of North Carolina. I cannot believe that all of this has been undertaken merely to give this school's graduates an economic advantage in the life struggle. "A university," said Professor Woodrow Wilson, "should be an organ of memory for the state, for the transmission of its best traditions." And Prince Bismarck was even more specific: "One-third of the students of German universities," he once stated, "broke down from over-work; another third broke down from dissipation; and the other third ruled Germany."

I leave it to each of you to decide in which category you will fall. I do not suggest that our political and public lives should be turned over to college-trained experts; nor would I give this university a seat in the Congress, as William and Mary was once represented in the Virginia House of Burgesses; nor would I adopt from the Belgian Constitution a provision giving three votes instead of one to college graduates—at least not until more Democrats go to college.

This university produces trained men and women, and what this country needs are those who look, as the motto of your state says, at things as they are and not at things as they seem to be. Our task in this country is to do our best to serve our nation's interests as we see them, and not to be swayed from our course by the faint-hearted or the unknowing or the threats of those who would make themselves our foes. This is not a simple task in a democracy.

Peace and freedom do not come cheap. We are destined, all of us here today, to live out most if not all of our lives in uncertainty and challenge and peril. Our policy must therefore blend whatever degree of firmness and flexibility which are necessary to protect our vital interest, by peaceful means if possible, by resolute action if necessary. There is, of course, no place in America where reason and firmness are more clearly pointed out than here in North Carolina.

We move for the first time in our history through an age in which two opposing powers have the capacity to destroy each other, and while we do not intend to see the free world give up, we shall make every effort to prevent the world from being blown up. The American eagle, on our official seal, emphasizes both peace and freedom, and as I said in the State of the Union address, we in this country give equal attention to its claws when in its left hand it holds the arrow and in its right the olive branch.

This is a time of national maturity and understanding and willingness to face issues as they are, not as we would like them to be. It is a test of our ability to be far-seeing and calm as well as resolute, to keep an eye on both our dangers and our opportunities, and not to be diverted by momentary gains or set-backs or pressures. It is the long view of the educated citizen to which the graduates of this university can best contribute. We must distinguish the real from the illusory, the long-range from the temporary, the significant from the petty. If we can face up to our risks and live up to our word, if we can do our duty, undeterred by fanatics or frenzy at home or abroad, then surely peace and freedom can prevail. We shall be neither red nor dead, but alive and free and worthy of the traditions and responsibilities of North Carolina and the United States of America.

ON LEAVING HIGH SCHOOL
AND HEADING FOR CHAPEL HILL

by Maggie Palmer Lauterer

I remember getting ready for my trip down the mountains to Chapel Hill. I had been accepted at the University that spring, and now, with summer coming on, it was time to begin gathering up all that was me to take off to college.

I needed a container. It just didn't seem right to go to a store and buy a tin and cardboard foot locker. There were more miles between home and the University then than there are now, and a lot more hours. I needed more sensible armor.

I remember walking across the orchard to my grandmother's old house. I climbed the stairs and began looking through the slanted, under-the-roof closets where I had played as a child. There were cobwebby trunks and suitcases there, used by aunts and uncles who had braved their own first days of college life, but it was in the dimly lit closet of the sleeping porch that I found my trunk.

The trunk was dark and dusty, and shreds of old canvas were peeling in patches across its arched top. Rusty metal straps ran down its sides, and the lock didn't work. Inside, the covering was tattered past the point of color or design.

The trunk had belonged to my grandfather, Grandmother told me, as she rubbed her fingers across its dusty lid. In it he had gathered up his belongings to carry them to a mountain school when our county had none. The trunk had been waiting in that closet for me, she said, "for the last 60 years."

Through the summer, after work, I'd labor for hours over that old trunk. I carefully cut away the rotting canvas to expose old, mellow pine sides. I sanded the wood to smoothness and the metal to brightness. I replaced the old shredded interior cloth with new fabric to make it ready for my "new life."

Then summer came to an end and I began to carefully pack my belongings. Everything fit. There was even room to spare as the heavy old lid settled firmly into place. Good thing: The old latch didn't work anyway.

I was nearly paralyzed with fear when Mom, Dad, and I arrived at McIver Hall in Chapel Hill. The big old dorm was bigger than my high school and housed more girls than there were inhabitants of my mountain village.

Mom nudged me out of the car while Dad opened the car trunk.

My room was on the third floor. Dad wrestled Granddad's old trunk to chest level and carried it up the winding stairwell. With a final puff, he gently set the trunk at the foot of a single metal bed by a window, where it would sit until I graduated.

There weren't many of us there from the mountains of North Carolina, and we soon found each other. But where we were from mattered less and less. We had become part of something bigger, and fear left us as familiarity arrived.

I learned a lot in those years—and only part of it in the classroom. I learned that fall meant "Hark the Sound" drifting from the Bell Tower after football games. I learned that spring meant flower ladies with bouquets of daffodils down on Franklin Street. I learned that Lenoir Hall was the best place for a cheap, but well-balanced, meal. I learned that a sunrise can bring dread on the morning of a final exam.

I learned lots of things, but I didn't know how much I had learned until it was time to leave.

Then one day I won my meek B.A. degree and started packing the old trunk, but everything would not fit. The lid wouldn't begin to come down, even when I put my weight on the top and pushed until the hinges creaked.

Granddad's old trunk came back to the mountains with me. So did a bunch of cardboard boxes that I had gathered up at Fowler's Grocery. The boxes carried all the things that I had become, all of the things that would not fit inside the trunk.

I guess I was a lot like that old trunk. I was too full of new knowledge, much of it about myself. Cherished knowledge becomes more and more important to me as the years go by. The cardboard boxes are gone now, and the things they held are scattered here and there. But I've still got the old trunk and the things I learned and became in Chapel Hill.

Alex Webb

"...Spring meant flower ladies with bouquets of daffodils down on Franklin Street."

THE CAROLINA COED

by Maggie Palmer Lauterer

For goodness sakes, how could there be a book about the Carolina experience without a few words about the Carolina coed?

The notion of a good education for young men is an old one, and we all know that the University was founded some 200 years ago for that very purpose. But it was well over a hundred years into its existence that the first woman graduated from Carolina. Mary MacRae was THE woman student in 1895. That didn't exactly open the floodgates to let women through.

In the mid 1960's, when I came to Chapel Hill, freshmen women were just beginning to be accepted in the general college, and the number of women transferring was on the increase. Still, there were six men to every woman student.

We were a minority and, indeed, we were treated like one. I remember cartoons of the Carolina coed in the *Daily Tar Heel,* drawn by a future Pulitzer Prize-winner, Jeff MacNelly. She was an airhead dressed in the coed "uniform": an A-line skirt, a blouse with a Peter Pan collar, penny loafers, and covering it all with a London Fog raincoat.

There was some disdain of the minority female at Carolina, but there was a bright side, too. Nature being as it is, the campus men found us to be suitable companions for football games, pizza at the Rat, and strolls in the Arboretum. Some of those Carolina Gentlemen actually asked some of us to become their wives.

Through it all, however, it was understood that we would remember our place. We were, after all, most appreciated for our blonde homecoming queens and our decorative presence at fraternity parties.

Those days of education at Carolina, however, were not lost on us. Many of my female cohorts have gone on to make a mark on the world. This minority fought for what we got, and what many of us won were doctorates, authorship and leadership.

Things are different now, or so I am told. There are now more women than men enrolled at the University. The young coed now dresses any way she damn well pleases and takes her place in the competitive arenas of school and business.

But it's still the men's basketball team that the world watches and it's still a pretty girl that wears the homecoming crown. We've come a long way, but......

NC Collection

Wash-dry-fold, Chapel Hill-style, 1948.

The 1951 May Court.

Ever chic, the Carolina coed of 1959 was admired for setting fashion trends, including adornment with tear-drop sunglasses.

WE CAME TO CAMELOT AND STAYED

by A.C. Snow

When our oldest daughter was small I would take her to Chapel Hill to see the Tar Heels play. By some incredible chance, we always went on days that were fair and fine, when Kenan swelled with "Hark the Sound" and the Bell Tower chimed the sweet melody of victory more times than not.

So, one October morn, when we set out for the game in the rain, the child was disconsolate.

"Don't worry," I said. "It never rains in Camelot." As if by miracle, when we came to those big blue heels painted on the pavement of N.C. 54 just outside the town, the rain stopped and then sun broke through.

Our daughter, already caught up in the magic of the place, vowed anew that at whatever cost she would go to school in Camelot. That dream, and her father's reminder when she dallied at her school work that, "You won't ever get into Camelot that way," drove her on to the grade point average that admitted her to UNC many years later.

Chapel Hill is Camelot to many, but to each generation it is a different place and time from the generation before or the one to follow. But the magnetic appeal of the place somehow is the same, enslaving us all throughout our small eternity there beneath the old oaks, along the well-worn paths, beside the Old Well and within the ivied halls.

Mine were the days of young ladies screaming "Man on the hall!" at Alderman and McIver, of spring stirring in the loins of youth, of moonlight and dogwoods in bloom, as someone said, "like bridesmaids walking to a wedding." Of frustrations you would expect on a campus of 7,000 men vying for the attention of 800 cruelly-discriminating women.

Some things never change; some do. On a recent stroll past the statue of Silent Sam, I found a checkbook some student had dropped in his rush to class. I inspected it so that I might return it to its rightful owner. To my astonishment it showed a balance of $2,158! In my day, that would have paid for two full years of tuition, room, board and allowance.

Student affluence is only a part of the lifestyle gap between my own and our children's time at Chapel Hill. A bed, a chair, a bureau—those were the furnishings of my 201 Lewis Dormitory room. Today, in our daughter's two-person room at Spencer Dorm, there are, in addition to those basics, a TV set, a stereo, a telephone, a "box" (slang for over-sized cassette player), a toaster oven, a refrigerator, an electric typewriter and a sewing machine.

In Chapel Hill, town and gown coexist in harmony, bound together by the same loyalty and love of the place. One of my favorite anecdotes has to do with the 5-year-old son of a UNC professor.

The boy was telling his mother how he and his little friends had conducted a funeral for a dead robin they had found on the lawn.

"We dug a little grave and we put the bird in it and we laid a big leaf over it and then we covered it up with dirt," the lad reported. "And we put up a stick for a tombstone. And then we sang a song."

"And what did you sing?" the mother asked curiously.

"We sung, 'We Don't Give a Damn for Duke University,' cause that was the only song all of us knowed."

Over the years, Carolina students have felt the acute pain of breaking the umbilical cord between alma mater's comfortable womb and the waiting world, with all its uncertainties, and the harsh realities of work and family and responsibility. Many of us survive the transition by clinging to the dream that here we will come again someday, perhaps to stay.

That dream consumed me early on. While still a student, I emptied an old sock of savings from meager Air Force pay in the South Pacific and plunked down $250 for a hard-scrabble quarter-acre on, where else, Charlie Justice Street. A few years later, when Carolina fever had subsided to the level of common sense, I sold the real estate for $800. But even now, my impractical heart keeps whispering that I will go home again.

Tom Wolfe, UNC's most hallowed literary son, felt that pain of farewell in *"Look Homeward Angel."* Driving away from the campus for the last time, "Eugene gave a great cry of pain and sadness, for he knew that the elfin door had closed behind him, and that he would never come back again."

In his painful parting, Tom Wolfe spoke for each of us. But he neglected to mention that most of us never really leave the Hill, at least not in the spiritual way that matters most.

The few inches of snow have covered the cemetery markers.

But they're still holding classes today...so start walking.

Snow flies both naturally and from the hands of snowball pitchers at Mangum, one of 30 residence halls.

Carroll Hall, the Business Administration building, wears a layer of winter white. Named for Dudley DeWitt Carroll, first dean of the School of Commerce, it corresponds in architecture to nearby Manning Hall.

C.J. . . . "the Shark."

I MAJORED IN ENGLISH OF A DIFFERENT KIND

by C.J. Underwood

Oh, if the walls of the Graham Memorial pool room could only talk!!

I was the *original* nerd…I mean, the real thing: horn-rimmed glasses, flat-top haircut, and 145 pounds of pure Squaresville. I would not have written this story had the editor of this book, a longtime friend, not insisted that the truth emerge in print after all these years of silence. He reminded me of baseball great Dizzy Dean's words for the ages: "Braggin' ain't braggin' if you can prove it." Dear reader, think me not a braggart as I tell you of a teenage hobby I sort of accidentally stumbled into. It was a hobby that became infinitely profitable to me in that I looked so nerdy. Who would have ever suspected that lurking behind the exiguous exterior of this Barney Fife look-alike was a veritable panther waiting to pounce on unsuspecting poolroom prey?

There is this little room, see, in the basement of the Graham Memorial Student Union, a room which at the time housed four very crooked, unbalanced, holey billiard tables. How was I to know that *first,* yes first, fearful day of college that for the next four years this would be my home? And it started out so innocently: "Hey, Underwood, you play nine-ball?" The question was akin to a lawyer being asked if he'd like to handle a Hollywood divorce.

"Well, gee, I guess I could try one game maybe for, say, fifty cents."

There began the longest continuing pool game in Orange County history, according to the 30 or so students who took me on during the next 12 hours. The only reason we quit was because they closed the place at midnight. Believe me, I really had intended to go to Orientation that afternoon and evening, but I just kept getting those lucky rolls. If my Momma knew how much money I won that day, and that week, she would've withdrawn me from the University and would have brought me back under her thumb in Raleigh.

To protect the innocent and defeated I will not mention the first name of a certain Mr. Thompson, a fellow student who helped support me through those next four years. If he reads this I know he will smile at the memory of my sweetest victory, the one that he watched at no charge (for a change). The fellow was big and muscular and from (Oh, I love it!) *Notre Dame.* A jock, no less, who had several hours to kill before boarding the bus for South Bend.

I can still see him sizing up The Nerd. He was three times my size, and the cue looked like a toothpick in his hands. "Got anybody around here who might want to play for ten bucks a game?" he asked, not noticing that my heart was fluttering uncontrollably under my "Beat Dook" T-shirt.

I choked and coughed and hesitatingly nodded in the affirmative as I fixed my mind on a Carolina blue wool sweater that was waiting for me in the window down at Milton's—just two blocks away. I had admired it many times as I passed their storefront, but I knew it would take several weeks of "quarter games" to earn enough to buy it.

"On second thought," I sputtered, "maybe you'd better give me a two-ball advantage. I'm not very good at this stuff."

"You're on," said he, fighting back a big, wide grin.

I still have that blue sweater, even though the coat and slacks and shoes that fellow paid for went out of style by my junior year. There is a happy academic ending, too. I actually spent enough time studying *real* English—the kind *without* topspin on it—to be ready for a real job in the outside world. I still miss those rickety, slanted old tables. The memories just get better and better, though, every time I put on that Carolina blue sweater.

Dr. G.V. Taylor

OUR PROFESSORS: HOW FORTUNATE WE WERE TO HAVE THEM SHARE THEIR LIVES WITH US

by Gray Temple, Jr.

Dr. Kenneth Reckford

Prior to entering Carolina, I spent five years in a Yankee prep school, a competitive, all-male setting in which one learned not by asking questions (betraying ignorance) but by making statements and defending them against all comers. It was a bit like half a decade in a submarine with a debate team.

Three years later I returned briefly. That visit differed from a recurring "Return to Massachusetts" nightmare in one detail: it was voluntary. I had not been snatched back to finish an incomplete Math course; rather, the school had requested that someone come up to represent UNC. Otherwise the scene reproduced the dream: it was nighttime, mid-winter, in the school library filled with skeptical faces. The audience comprised boys who had been enrolled at Harvard within five minutes of an obstetrician announcing their arrival and sex.

"How many courses are you taking this semester?" asked one.

"Six," I replied.

"Of those six, how many do you actually enjoy?" he asked, lots of topspin on "actually."

"Oh, maybe five," I responded after embarrassed calculation.

He responded with a graceless grin. Anger carromed about my abdomen, felt for the implied dishonor to professors and instructors worthy of admiration.

They flashed through my mind that moment. It won't be difficult to recall them; they are with me yet.

First, unnamed but ever-loved, my Zoology lab instructor. A buxom redhead, cheerful, delighting in matters biological, she would press her blushing cheek against mine, arm and ample bosom draped about my left shoulder, right eye to the left eye-piece of my microscope, explaining things from that position in gratifying detail, a generous response to one recently released from prep school.

After 27 years, I still feel cheery at the thought of a paramecium.

I thought of my Greek professor, Dr. Kenneth Reckford, the Monday morning in 1962 when the Cuban Missile Crisis peaked. Away for the weekend, Dr. Reckford had been unaware of our nation's peril. Entering the classroom, he glimpsed a newspaper headline left on a desk, grabbed it, read it with deepening concern, murmuring, "This is terrible, dreadful."

Scrapping his lecture, he spoke of nations abdicating their freedom by allowing politicians to redefine important words: words like "peace," "honor," "freedom," "truth." He quoted lengthily from Thucydides—intoning the Greek text, extending its urgency to us across 2400 years.

At the bell, each student was changed: no longer anxious Jingoists, but grieving patriots.

I thought of Dr. G.V. Taylor teaching Western Civ. I once dared challenge him on a trivial detail. Rather than roar, he beamed:

"Let's *both* study that, Mr. Temple, and see who's right; if you are correct, I will give you…let's see…a cigar!"

Two days later, he presented the cigar with a courtly flourish and grinned in my direction as I smoked it to the stub.

That generous gesture left us all eager to work harder for him. What rewards might be in store?

The Chairman of the Classics Department was Dr. Albert Suskin, a short, leonine presence of unimpeachable dignity and hooded—but merry—eyes.

Speaking of Catullus' contempt for bad writing:

"That antipathy I share," quoth he; "I have discouraged any number of students from bad writing."

"But Dr. Suskin," complained a candidate for that ministration, "most people have bad taste; shouldn't there be writers for them?"

With no visible movement of face or body he seemed to swell before us. His reply rumbled down as from Olympus:

"Such people are not our present concern."

Only the slightest wink betrayed his meaning: "Be the best you can be and require no excuses."

Dr. Albert Irving Suskin

Spying my former German teacher in the library, I thought of the difficulty a fellow undergraduate experienced grasping the German subjunctive. Dr. Ransom Taylor settled it in his deadpan, Peter Lorre manner:

"God shave the Queen!"

German took on the charm of its professor.

I thought of Dr. Harold McCurdy's demanding but popular "Personality Psychology" course. It was the early sixties; most of us were white and our inherited segregationist notions had not come under scrutiny.

One week he spoke of the Super-Ego (the "conscience" to most of us). With tear-filled eyes he urged us to "filter parents out of our super-egos." The voice of conscience is not the voice of God. He characterized the walls frustrating our ideals as paper stage-props maintained by moral cowardice, insisting that we leave no obstacle untested.

I had little interest in divinity studies then. Yet the moral power of truthful public speech was conceived in me at that hour. Many there became active in the Integration struggle in subsequent months.

These men and women—and others—passed before me that night in New England as the student asked his question, "How many do you actually enjoy?"

Dr. Harold McCurdy

A Master present (who had done graduate study at Carolina!) forestalled my response:

"You cannot realize what a high proportion five out of six is. At an Ivy League school you first meet professors in graduate school. Few of you will have such relationships with your instructors."

I felt a rush of gratitude to him, a teacher who knew the sound of good teaching by its echo.

All I knew then was that my teachers at Chapel Hill were special to me because they had taught me that real learning is not based on competition and disdain. In later years I have measured them against the faculties of four academies in as many countries where I studied or taught. Even in this varied company, they prevail—wonderfully colorful, humane, and most likely to lose sleep over an idea.

I REMEMBER THE RAINS

by Julian Scheer

The day I first set foot in Chapel Hill, it was raining. The driver who had given the hitchhiker a ride pulled his car to the curb in front of Ab's tobacco row bookshop on Franklin Street and I climbed out, pulling an old suitcase behind me—a suitcase with several pairs of worn, wartime khaki trousers, a few leftover T-shirts, a couple of books and a box of homemade candy.

I ran beneath the awning to get out of the shower. A record player blasted music into the street and I half listened as I surveyed the scene about me. Under every tree, it seemed, were students and townsfolks, not a single one with a raincoat. They stood waiting for the rain to stop.

Suddenly the shower was over, and people began to move again, spreading out on the walks and moving quickly to make up for lost time. There was a sudden, herky-jerky atmosphere like the fast frames of silent film days—people quick-stepping to their destinations. I asked directions from a rather loud, friendly man, who later turned out to be named Kemp Nye and who seemed to know that I (a complete stranger) was coming. Kemp appeared to be the town host, and he headed me toward a boarding house on Mallette Street.

Before I reached my destination, it had showered once or twice more and I, too, ducked beneath awnings or trees and had, I realized later, taken the first step toward becoming a native.

It rained a lot that fall. And in the spring, too, and when you think of Chapel Hill, you've got to remember the rain.

And the long walks across the campus on soggy, sandy walks, hundreds of students hunched over, keeping rain from the skies and drippings from the trees from trickling down their collars by covering themselves with the *Daily Tar Heel*, heads down, walking, hurrying, hurrying, hurrying.

And the smell of classes, especially those in the frame barracks buildings which bordered the campus in the post-war years. In the spring, like wet dogs. Of course, there was usually a wet dog in the classroom, curled beneath a desk or shaking himself on unguarded students. The wet coats and hats and damp trouser cuffs—these odors mixed with the green outdoor aroma or the steamy vapors from the hot rooftops.

It used to rain, often. And no one seemed ready for it. Ever. There was a line in one of the catalogues which suggested one bring raincoats and boots, but no one seemed to have read it. There was only the un-umbrellaed student and his equally unprepared teacher—both scurrying to class or office, rushing to roll up car windows, pulling frantically on convertible tops, male students jamming books inside their shirts next to the skin to keep them dry, and female students using their books as hats to keep Friday night hairdos intact.

And rain made it a better day for the Carolina or Varsity movie theaters, or to drink a beer at Brack Creel's place, or to sit on fraternity house porches.

In winter there was no rain quite like Chapel Hill's, it seemed, for nipping noses and ears, or for getting deep inside bones, or for making the closeness almost unbearable, although it made a silver-shiny picture and made a lightly noisy song as the drippings hit piles of reddened winter leaves.

It ruined things, too. Like nights at Kenan Dorm or football games, Hogan's Lake, or blueberry picking at Phillips Russell's place, but, oddly, I don't remember the rain as being much of a conversation piece. It was taken for granted, this rain. This eternal Chapel Hill rain.

But I remember it vividly even today.

The heat of the Dean Dome is the surest cure for the Rainy Day Chapel Hill Blues.

OF HOTPLATES, HARRY'S AND LENOIR HALL

by Jim Jenkins

It is my nearly religious belief, and the absolutely factual claim of what follows, that there is a factor in the making of a Carolina gentleman, a compleat man, often ignored by those who engage in long and misty remembrances of Chapel Hill. So let us dispense with lyrical essays about the wonders of the city and the old school thereabouts, and get down to something really important: food. For, if college and Chapel Hill represent the age at which a young man enjoys-endures-suffers his first separation from the coziness of his home hearth, the serenity of his own room and the dependability of his father's car, it means also the most traumatic separation of all—the parting of ways with his mother's kitchen.

This is a grievous situation indeed, brought home to me the first time I entered a room in Grimes dormitory to room with a raw-boned fellow named Merlin Young, who stored in the second drawer of his bureau a hotplate encrusted with the memories of his personal haute cuisine. The cord was patched with Scotch tape, except where the tape had come loose and the copper was hanging out. The first time I met Merlin, he sized me up carefully, making sure I was not the dorm inspector, who often came in search of illegal hotplates, and once he'd determined my identity, offered me the use of his fry pan, so long as I agreed to wipe it out with anything except his towels. The use of a hotplate, and the ability to use one without coming down with some mysterious strain of poisoning, was my first lesson in becoming a compleat man.

The second lesson came in Harry's, that long-lost Chapel Hill monument now occupied by a restaurant named after Dean Smith's basketball offense and featuring sandwiches named after his players. But when Harry's was Harry's, we were served therein by long-haired kids in tie-dyed T-shirts who gave you the opportunity to place an order not with one of those sickening salutations, "Hi, I'm Mandy, and I'll be your hostess today…" but instead with "Yeah, whatcha want, man?" My personal favorite was the hot roast turkey, which was two slices of processed turkey on white bread covered with gravy and half-cooked French Fries. When you had reached that station in life where the Harry's people knew your usual, you were one step closer to compleat.

This brings me to the Porthole, which of course brings me immediately to the Porthole rolls. Exquisite, soft and tasty, they had people lining up outside and willingly waiting for half an hour for the opportunity to butter one up. A man who knew of Porthole rolls had achieved one more rung on the ladder of sophistication and breeding.

And now, The Zoom. The Zoom Zoom was yet another Franklin Street haven to which students would repair in the company of a date or shortly after their monthly expense allowances arrived. The steaks were thick, tasty, and wonderfully greasy, so that clean-shaven students needed to consume them with great care and the bearded ones could relive the Zoom experience for hours thereafter.

Likewise at the Rathskeller, another place which picked up whenever parents were in town or had sent along a greenback remembrance. It was, however, a dangerous economic venture for a man with date in tow, as he could expect to live on peanut butter crackers and the water fountain for some days or weeks thereafter.

All of these places were essentially escapes from that least-desirable of all alternatives, Student Food. This institution had been feared for its quality and yet appreciated for its economy since the days of the Great Depression, when a full meal was 35 cents and grits were one penny. It was something of a tradition to criticize student food, even on those days when it wasn't half bad. When the student food service was located in Swain Hall, it was unaffectionately referred to as "Swine Hall." When it was in Lenoir Hall, that spot was dubbed Lean over the Rail Hall or the Ptomaine Cafe. In fact, the fare in those places was probably more healthful than that served in the more glamorous spots on Franklin Street.

And speaking of healthful, there is one final point of which all those of my generation can be proud. The phenomenon of health food—that mixture of inedible fruits, nuts and salads which look like new-mown grass—was blessedly absent in the Chapel Hill of that day. Sprouts were something we shaved off in the morning. Yogurt was a distant memory of reading *Heidi.* And health food was ordering the baked potato instead of the fries at the Zoom.

Danziger's Restaurant, site of 10,000 budding romances.

THE TOWN HAS CHANGED, BUT IT IS STILL VERY SPECIAL

by Woody Durham

"I'm so jealous that you've already gotten back to Chapel Hill."

It was spring of 1984, and I listened to those words coming at me over the telephone as I sat gazing out my office window at the Village Companies off Weaver Dairy Road. On the line was a carpet executive in north Georgia who has been a close friend since our undergraduate days at the University in the early 1960's.

Now—21 years later—my association with the Tar Heel Sports Network had brought me back to the Southern part of heaven. Yet, growing up with relatives in the immediate area, coming over from Greensboro or Raleigh-Durham on frequent television assignments through the years, and working as the "Voice of the Tar Heels" made me feel as if a part of me had always been in Chapel Hill.

Again, on a regular basis, I would be able to stroll down Franklin Street, eat at the Rat, walk across campus, and perhaps even monitor a few classes. It would be just like it used to be when I was in school at Carolina. At least, I thought so. I didn't think about all of the changes since 1963.

Roland Giduz, a former newspaper reporter turned writer, came to Chapel Hill as an infant more than 60 years ago when his father arrived to teach French at UNC. He claims, "Change is the only constant in a University town."

A growing University dictated a lot of changes, and most of its growth came during the 1960's. Prompted by the admission of freshmen women shortly after my graduation, an additional 1,000 students started coming each year. The population of the community swelled from 12,500 to its current total of more than 35,800. It is projected at better than 43,000 by 1990.

A lot of those people are UNC graduates who just can't face the reality of leaving the area. Others are newcomers to the Research Triangle Park, which becomes even more accessible with the opening of I-40, and it has certainly given a broader dimension to the uniqueness of the community. And, still others are part of an ever-growing retirement colony. As the University grew, with women now accounting for 60 percent of its 22,000-plus enrollment, the town of Chapel Hill grew and became more of a community in its own right. Even adjacent Carrboro emerged in the mid-1970's as its own vigorous entity.

Of course, there are a few people not willing to accept the growth and change, but most of the long-time residents were receptive. Yet, they still hold a certain nostalgia for the village atmosphere as it once existed.

Giduz doesn't believe all aspects of such an atmosphere have been lost, but Sandy McClamroch, who was Mayor of Chapel Hill during the turbulent integration period of the 1960's, thinks it is gone. "That stretch of Franklin from Columbia down to the post office is the area most of the alums remember," he points out. "And, there is a certain charm still evident, but the rest has grown a lot and is spread out all over hell." In the late 1960's alone more than $32 million was spent on construction as the NCNB Plaza became a dominant structure on Franklin Street. A flood of protest signatures limited the building to three stories on Franklin, but it rises to six floors back on Rosemary Street.

Now Rosemary Square has been approved, and it will change the appearance of the downtown area even more.

The surrounding area is dotted by clusters of apartments on just about every corner or in every available space. "Density" has become a rather dirty word because the growth, while healthy for new input, should have been better controlled. Giduz contends, "The leadership of the community is now trying to slow down the growth, but its efforts have been difficult to enforce." However, he does believe the "horizons" for most people are still at the village level. "Protecting trees and dogs is more than a casual idea," Giduz feels. He honestly thinks the congestion around Chapel Hill could be worse. Long-range planning has finally been put into motion, and Pittsboro Street is one-way going south past the Carolina

Raising money for the cause of education has taken some interesting twists during the University's first 200 years.

Inn with Columbia Street one-way coming back north from the medical complex. It's possible Franklin Street will eventually be turned into one-way heading east, while Rosemary Street will be used as the western outlet.

As the community has changed another long-time Chapel Hill resident feels the ambience of the UNC campus has disappeared. Claudia Cannady says, "High buildings dominate the scenery, and they hide traditional landmarks such as the Bell Tower. And practically every open area has been paved for parking." She finds it difficult to now walk straight across the campus, which has Kenan Stadium as its centerpiece.

Yet, despite all of the growth which has brought about considerable change, both the town and the University remain very special places with unique appeal. Why?

Even though it might not still have the village atmosphere of years ago, Chapel Hill remains the home of the University, and despite the physical changes there is still that feeling about the place I came to love as a student. And I'm enjoying it again as a resident.

It's very evident that those who come now as students, or those former students like me who are fortunate enough to return, are all just so happy to be here. That makes it easier to understand why others want to come back someday, perhaps permanently.

Which is what my Georgia friend was telling me.

NC Collection

Thomas Dunstan, nineteenth century Chapel Hill barber and businessman.

A cool drink from the original Old Well.

NC Collection

The picture tells it all:
Charlie Scott, happy scholar.

Hugh Morton

GREAT SCOTT!

by Hugh Morton, Jr.

Charles Thomas Scott, by word and example, co-authored a new era in the Saga of the South. To simply write of him as one of the University's most gifted athletes, or as the first Black to play a major sport in the Land of Cotton, or as the teenage Harlem pilgrim who arrived in Chapel Hill via a road untravelled, would be to fall short of honoring this man with the place he deserves in our school's history.

His father died when Charlie was 14—a tragedy that by itself would raise to staggering proportions the odds against his even staying *in* school, much less graduating from high school as *Valedictorian,* no less. For that honor he says he will be forever indebted to his mother, his teachers, and friends like Mrs. Evelyn Jarrett and Mr. and Mrs. Frank McDuffie.

The South of the early and middle sixties was comprised of a folk who didn't know exactly what they believed or where things were going; many, if not most, whites were afraid of change. There were riots, demonstrations, "sit-ins," and marches. History shows us that nearly every instance of "trouble" involved peaceful Blacks being confronted by intolerant, hostile whites. Still, it came as a painful shock when two of Charlie's best friends were denied service at a North Carolina college-town restaurant. Thankfully, that town wasn't Chapel Hill.

As his classmate I saw in Charlie several "superlatives" not listed in the record books: He was a brilliant student who won Academic All-American honors by studying when others were sleeping; he was as humble and friendly as anyone on campus; and he endured an *enormous* amount of pressure. It would serve no useful purpose to print here the words some opponents' fans yelled at him, but be assured that those racial slurs could not have been borne on the shoulders of anyone less than a Man's Man.

For the record, here is what was accomplished by the most graceful athlete who ever donned a sky-blue jersey: First-team All-America in 1969 and 1970 and three-time All-ACC choice; second-leading scorer (2,007 points), second-leading assist-maker, and leading rebounder (for his size, that is) among UNC players with only three varsity seasons; UNC's second-highest single-season scorer (27.1 points per game); ACC Tournament MVP and championship game scoring record-holder (40 points); MVP of the Eastern Regionals; and ACC Athlete of the Year.

He traded #33 for other uniforms and more records: Olympic Gold Medalist (1968); 30.6 scoring average in two ABA seasons; 25+ scoring average in four seasons with the Phoenix Suns; a three-year average of nearly 18 points per game with the champion Boston Celtics; and five times an NBA All-Star.

His greatest gifts, though, were not his soft jump shot and his kangaroo's spring, but unselfish humility, a quick, broad smile, and an insistence on thanking everyone who helped him make all those A's and B's and score all those points. At a time in his life and during an age in our nation when giving must have seemed difficult, Charles Thomas Scott gave to the University all that one can give. Seventeen years after his graduation it seems appropriate that we give back to him a warm and gracious, "Thank you, Charlie."

Charles Scott, graceful as a greyhound with the spring of a jackrabbit, left many defenders flat-footed and mesmerized by his aerial antics.

MEMORIES

by Charles T. Scott

The sixth of September, 1986, was a magical day in my life. As I walked through the doors of the Dean E. Smith Center to play in the alumni basketball game, the years seemed to fade. . . almost as if it were 1966 again. I thought back to the sounds of Carmichael, to the nets we cut down in Greensboro, Charlotte and elsewhere, but mostly my memories were of the people who made it all possible.

The year 1966-67—that difficult time of making the adjustment from high school to college—was made so much easier for me by Coach Smith, Coach Lotz, and so many others. Coach Smith, in fact, treated me so fairly that he ruined me for life, and as for Coach Lotz, he was best man in my wedding—that tells you how much I think of him.

The 1967-68 and 1968-69 seasons were great ones if you're a Tar Heel fan. I had the assignment of filling the shoes of Bobby Lewis, that great All-American who still holds the UNC single-game scoring record (49 points). Fortunately, in 1967-68 we had four fabulous returning starters: All-American Larry Miller, who later scored 77 points in a pro game; Dr. Franklin St. Clair Clark, the Fayetteville physician who was known then as "Rusty"; Dick Grubar, for whom the "Four Corners" offense might have been invented; and Bill Bunting, a great team player, defender and rebounder.

Those friends, plus Coach Guthridge, Joe Brown, Gerald Tuttle, Eddie Fogler, Jim Delany, Ricky Webb and so many others, made my first year on the varsity easy because of the way they accepted me and helped me. In 1968 and 1969 we won 55 games and lost nine; won ACC and Eastern Regional championships both years; and finished second in the nation in 1968 only because Lew Alcindor was UCLA's center, and we played them in Los Angeles instead of Chapel Hill.

I thank all of my coaches and teammates for making me look good enough to get a tryout with the 1968 Olympic team. Winning a Gold Medal was, of course, a thrill that defies description.

The entire community of Chapel Hill and many others across the state reached out to me during those years and made me feel loved and appreciated. There are too many to properly thank here, but I especially want to mention James and Tassie Dempsey of Wilson, former All-American Lee Shaffer, and my roommate, Randy Forehand. Great people. While there were still some racial problems in the state when I graduated in 1970, they were problems that were at least being dealt with instead of being ignored.

It's September 6, 1986: Once again I'm running out of the dressing room and through the tunnel in a Tar Heel uniform, except this time onto a new court in a much bigger arena. As I gaze up into the rafters and see my jersey hanging beside those of Rosenbluth, Ford, Worthy, Jordan and others, I think back to the words of Carolina's former basketball announcer, Bill Currie, who said, "Nobody ever gets over being a Tar Heel." The thrill is still there. You're right, Bill, you never get over it.

Hugh Morton

*These Carolina gentlemen had the impossible task of
following the basketball act of 1957: Shaffer, Larese,
Salz and Moe.*

High-scoring 'Heels: All-Americans Larry Miller (left) and Bob Lewis (center) hold high one of the many trophies they captured with Tom Gauntlett (right), Rusty Clark, Dick Grubar, Bill Bunting and others.

WE SHOWED THE NATION
OUR BEST VIA TELEVISION

by Smith Barrier

Hugh Morton

U.S. Senator Sam J. Ervin, Jr.

America watches television, hour after day after week after month. With dozens of new cable and satellite channels debuting each year, viewers are now faced with a glut of poor programming that is normally punctuated by uncreative writing and third-rate acting. Even amid such mediocrity, though, we as a University family can take pride in having offered the nation at least four distinguished alumni—certainly leaders in their chosen fields—who became friends with multimillions of us through the medium of television. I refer, of course, to "Senator Sam" Ervin, Sheriff Andy Taylor (Griffith), "On the Road" journalist Charles Kuralt, and "On the Air" acrobat Michael Jordan. The younger generation especially has grown up knowing and loving them: To many they *are* the University. Noble representatives, these four.

The late U.S. Senator Sam J. Ervin, Jr., our wily and witty "country lawyer" from Morganton, would've been the first to tell you that he was deeply saddened to become a celebrity, if you will, the way Fate choreographed it. It began May 13, 1973, in the Senate Caucus Room. Senator Ervin chaired the televised hearings of the Select Committee on Presidential Campaign Activities, more popularly known as the Senate "Watergate Committee."

Having served in the Senate for two decades, the Tar Heel raconteur, author and former judge was no novice at such things. In 1954 Ervin was part of the special Senate committee that studied the actions of one Senator Joseph McCarthy and his charges of Communism that had been leveled at a host of government officials. The Senate censured McCarthy; thus began Senator Sam's career as the nation's foremost defender of civil liberties, the protector immaculate of the U.S. Constitution.

Before his Watergate chair, full-center before the probing lenses of the television cameras, appeared Erlichman, Mitchell, Dean and Haldeman—each charged with discrepancies in the Nixon White House. With his mountain drawl, those homey homilies and a keen lawyer's interrogation, the televised hearings brought the good Senator into every home in the land. He quoted the Bible and William Pitt the Elder. His was indignant, though courtly, oratory against the Watergate conspirators. "Senator Sam": Conscience of the Senate and, in the eyes of many, the last of the Founding Fathers.

Sheriff Andy Taylor undoubtedly will serve longer than any elected or appointed official in American history. He's going to work again this morning, right there in Mayberry, somewhere near his hometown of Mount Airy. Sheriff Taylor is still in office because of reruns, a special campaign contribution few elected officials can claim.

The "Andy Griffith Show" began in 1960, and over its eight-year run in the nation's "Top 10" TV shows, it offered up 249 episodes of Opie, Barney, Aunt Bee, Floyd, Goober, Gomer and, of course, the Sheriff. It was another era. No sexual language or even words such as "crazy" or "prostitute" were allowed. The Sheriff was the funny man who, over time, became straighter and straighter as Deputy Barney developed into the high-strung, one-bullet-in-the-shirt-pocket character who always got locked in the cell, whether by hook or by crook. "Sheriff Taylor changed 180 degrees from where he started," Andy said some years later.

In the fifties Andy Griffith's first job was teaching in the Goldsboro schools, but he and his wife created a "civic club act" to help pay the bills. One ballad, "What It Was Was Football," was rendered at the Chapel Hill Kiwanis Club on a Ladies Night, and newspaperman and Kiwanian Orville Campbell quickly saw that what it was was hilarious. They produced a recording, and Andy's stock soared. There was the Ed Sullivan Show, then two movies, "Face in the Crowd" and "No Time for Sergeants."

But nothing can touch "Mayberry" and its pure, unadulterated corn—where right always wins and problems are always solved before the whistling sign-off. America liked the show so much that, even though Andy has a current, high-standing TV show called "Matlock," it is the original "Mayberry" show that shines brightest in the syndication sky.

Active today is the "Andy Griffith Show Rerun Watchers Club," with teenagers, college professors and journalists as members...comin' home to Mayberry one more time.

It's just as simple as this: Charles Kuralt loved to travel, enjoyed the average man and woman, and could tell a tale about them that made you feel as if you were in that family's dining room or cow barn. Kuralt, born in Wilmington but raised primarily in Charlotte left the University as editor of the 1955 *Daily Tar Heel* to become a newspaperman in the Queen City, but after winning the coveted Ernie Pyle Award before he was old enough to vote, he—like Andy—got "discovered."

Best of this teddy bear newsman's ventures, of course, was CBS' "On the Road" series that covered all 50 states. With his crew crammed into a motor van equipped with Vienna sausages, day-old Danish, typewriter and TV set, Kuralt would be giving you an interesting story from Cannonball, North Dakota, or Whynot, North Carolina. He once said of his travels to Small Town USA: "We try to keep the 'On the Road' travels as inefficient and unplanned as possible. When we run out of canned pork 'n' beans or instant coffee, we just pull over and buy some more. There's at least one great story to be found at every turn in the road."

The show began in 1967, they parked the van in the garage in 1980, and "CBS Sunday Morning" came to life with Kuralt as host. And not often enough we are treated to a national newscast which concludes with that down-home voice: "That's the CBS Evening News. I'm Charles Kuralt sitting in for Dan Rather."

Indeed, the man is versatile, and CBS knows that. The Kuralt of the future may be involved with prime-time news specials for CBS, which is contemplating a nostalgia news show that may be titled "The Way We Were."

"North Carolina Is My Home," on which he collaborated with Charlotte composer Loonis McGlohon, brings Kuralt—in record, tape and book form—to where his heart remains. Here is a man with an eye and a heart for everyday heroes. Asked what she likes most about her favorite TV journalist, my wife replies: "I trust him. I believe what he tells me."

Michael Jordan's eyes were lighting up under the glare of the Louisiana Superdome and 61,162 pairs of eyes, not counting a TV audience of millions. His Tar Heel basketball team and Georgetown were battling for the 1982 NCAA national championship, and there was no immediate, sure-fire conclusion in sight. The Hoyas lead by one...19 seconds on the big clock in the sky... the ball goes from Black to freshman Jordan... he jumps (very high)... shoots... *scores!* Carolina wins, 63-62!

It was made-for-television drama, and Jordan said in the New Orleans aftermath: "When I was on the bus coming over here from the hotel I thought about the possibility of my taking a shot that would win or lose the game. What if my last-second shot would determine how the game came out? I guess it was a premonition." It was far more than that—it was Jordan's one-way flight to Superstardom.

Since his prep days in Wilmington, people, educated *medical* people, have wondered how he stays suspended in midair for so long. People, basketball people, stand and applaud his leaps and stuffs and antics that defy nature. The NBA defense has not given up yet, but they all wave white flags when Michael's on the court. He led the league in scoring by a mile and polled more votes than any other for the 1987 All-Star game. Add to that list NCAA Player of the Year, Olympic Gold Medalist, NBA Playoff Game scoring leader, and NBA Slam-Dunk champion. Even his tongue hanging out makes highlight film.

"Air Jordan" was made for television. Even his Nike shoe commercials are unbelievable... for a human, that is.

Charles B. Kuralt

Dr. Roger Miller, associate professor of chemistry, demonstrates the Argon ion pumped dye laser which is being utilized for the study of metal clusters. These clusters mimic the surfaces of metals often used as catalysts in large-scale chemical operations.

In a physics honors research project, undergraduate Brad Turpin studies the structure of noncrystalline semiconductors by using the Argon laser.

Medical technologist Christine Barnett loads serum samples for enzyme testing on an RA-1000 centrifugal analyzer at North Carolina Memorial Hospital. Work in the Clinical Chemistry department of the hospital helps in monitoring patients who have experienced heart attacks and other traumas.

The imposing columns of Morehead Planetarium provide a sense of stability for this sunny scene of study time.

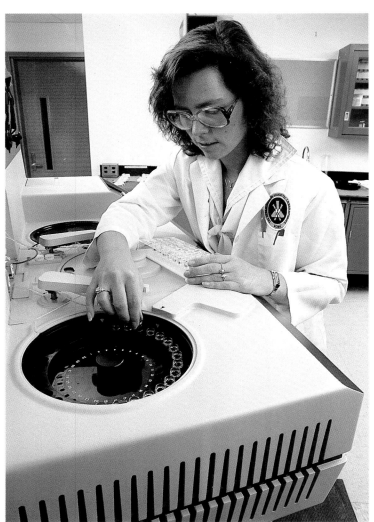

Incoming students must *know more than we did. Many of the concepts they will encounter as undergraduates—gene splicing and recombinant DNA, stereochemistry and conformational analysis, for example—did not even appear in my edition of Webster's Intercollegiate Dictionary. And the* opportunities *to study at Carolina have grown like a high-rise dormitory in the 34 years since I set my freshman foot on campus.*

Today's scholars enjoy certain advantages over my class. Back then we relied on slide rules, a species of student aid the computer made extinct, somewhere between the Apollo and Voyager space programs. When frugality failed us, we had to depend on carefully-worded letters to our parents for extra pocketmoney. Today's students just go to the nearest automated teller machine.

And the forest where Carolina ladies and gentlemen once "courted," is midcourt of a 22,000-seat athletic center. I must confess that as editor of the Daily Tar Heel, *I favored— editorially—withdrawing Carolina from big-time sports and the rigorous demands sports can make on the student-athlete. There wasn't much support for that. You simply cannot persuade 50,000 people to buy tickets to watch a student study.*

Charles Kuralt

Coaching can be a very active profession!

"THANK YOU, COACH SMITH, FOR BEING MY TEACHER, MY BROTHER AND MY FRIEND"

by Phil J. Ford, Jr.

Once or twice in a lifetime, if you're lucky, the good Lord directs your steps so that you'll cross paths with someone who'll prove to be a true friend—a man or woman with whom you can share anything and any problem. Such a person puts no demands or conditions on the friendship; it's never an "If you'll do this for me, I'll do this for you" kind of relationship. A good friend is never judgmental; a good friend is gifted at listening.

I thank God I have three such friends: two loving parents and Dean E. Smith.

I recall a thousand times when he demonstrated to me and my teammates that we were special, *really* special to him on a personal level, and that there is much, much more to life than a basketball game. One of the best examples was at the beginning of a big game when I was a freshman. Coach Smith and everyone else in the arena knew our team was up-tight because our pre-game shooting was awful. When we huddled before the tip-off he said, "Do you fellows realize that there are more than a *billion* people in China who will never know we played this game tonight? Now how about going out there and relaxing and having a good time."

Coach Smith has a unique recruiting philosophy that really caught me and my parents off-guard—a philosophy that underscores what a sensitive, caring man he truly is. He was the only coach who came to Rocky Mount and for a full hour never once brought up the subject of basketball. He talked to me about studying and graduating—subjects he came back to over and over again in the four years that followed. He talked about world hunger and race relations, but never once in that particular hour did he mention basketball.

Furthermore—and most people find this amazing—to my knowledge he's never promised any high school senior a starting spot on Carolina's varsity basketball team. Other coaches said, "Here's the ball, and it'll be all yours to do with what you wish for four years." Not Coach Smith. He talked about how important a college degree is if you want to get all you can out of yourself and get prepared to try and make the world better for others.

My first two games at Carolina were the worst I ever played, including my years in junior and senior high and the NBA. I made so many turnovers that people in Chapel Hill were saying, "Ford is an Edsel." Coach Smith stuck with me, even though we both knew I couldn't jump very high and I was slower than a lot of players my size. He kept reassuring me that although I was making some mistakes, they were what he called "good ideas."

His coaching philosophy is simple and consistent, year after year: Never be rude to or put down anyone; no one is more important than anyone else; train hard; prepare for any and all situations; think(!!); always keep yourself under control; play as fair and as smart as you can; and, win or lose, always be gracious and congratulate the other guy. I have found that those are also good rules for living when basketball is behind you.

Have you ever noticed that when his players are cutting down nets and signing autographs and whooping it up after a victory, Coach Smith is always in the background, smiling, but never out in the middle promoting himself? Have you ever heard him take credit for *anything*, even the smallest thing, related to a victory? Have you ever heard him blame a loss on anyone other than himself?

It must have been very difficult for him to tough it out with me when I had a serious personal problem after my seventh year in the NBA. After all, didn't he have enough to take care of in Chapel Hill without having to call me everyday to see how I was coming along with my recovery? That in itself was a lesson to me in what true friendship is all about.

I could tell from watching and listening to him during my years at Carolina that Coach Smith is a deeply spiritual man, but never did he force that side of his life on any of us players. He practiced it instead of preaching it, but we all knew it was there. When I started my life over again at age 29 I sought out the spiritual side of Coach Smith and found him to be an even sturdier rock than I thought he was. And what a blessing it is to know that he's always there.

Successful, gray-haired doctors, lawyers and businessmen who played under him 20 and 25 years ago tell me that they still seek his advice before making any serious career decisions. And he's always there for them, too, which is one reason why they're so successful. You see, his relationship with me is by no means unique. All of my teammates—and those who played before and after us—share these exact memories and sentiments.

I have thought long and hard about how I can summarize my feelings—our feelings—about this wonderful friend we have. One sentence won't do it, but I hope he'll accept this as the ultimate compliment: Coach Smith is the only man I ever met who has 154 children, and only four of them are girls.

Olympians, All-Americans, net bearers, NBA stars, and insepa-rable friends: Phil Ford (left) and Walter Davis.

Hugh Morton

THE DRAGON-SLAYERS, 1982

by Curry Kirkpatrick

Afterward. In the corner, against a wall stark in brick, two players sit vacantly, Jimmy Black, hand on chin, contemplating his knee; James Worthy, head bowed, hands clasped in supplication, the shreds of victory rope yet clinging to his dampened neck. Standing, waiting, their senses equally hollowed out, all of them trapped by the camera lens in a certain kind of exhausted, emotional paralysis, Dean Smith grimly stares at the floor, tongue gripped against upper lip, while Rick Brewer, the sports information director, cognizant that there may still be life out there on the planet, checks his watch. What time was it? It was about time... twenty-five years since the last time. What was the feeling? "The picture explained it better than words," Matt Doherty would say. "It was like... Whew! What the heck did we just go through?" And? "... and... thank God, it was... finally... over."

Aside from the fact that they stayed healthy, there wasn't much surface difference between the 1981-82 Tar Heels who finally won Coach Smith's first national championship and his six previous teams who had reached the NCAA Final Four and not won. Or the three or four who followed them and, uninjured, might have done the same thing. Yet as this star-touched crew traversed that bewitching season, emboldened from the Finals defeat of the previous March; reinvigorated as number one for most of the winter-spring; victors over the pretender Kentucky; rampagers of the ACC; slayers of the dragons Sampson and Ewing; a nifty, resourceful, sometimes spectacular and always multidimensional unit whose ability to play both fast and slow not only won games (32 of 34) but was to actually change the rules of the Game (effecting the advent of the shot clock)—who could deny these 'Heels were something very special?

There was the old McGuirean underground railway connection from New York: Black, Doherty and Sam Perkins vaguely knew each other amid Big Apple surroundings before coming to Chapel Hill. And the state itself contributed to the starting five a pair of natives not to mention absolute court genies, practically from the very breadth of its being: the nonpareil power man, Worthy, out of the textile mills of the west (Gastonia), the exquisite dreamfigure Michael Jordan, from near the craggy seashores of the east (Wilmington).

How strange the roots of a champion! Way back in a high school scrimmage Black deliberately tripped Doherty before getting in a fistfight with Matt's teammates; upon Doherty introducing himself to Perkins as being a fellow Tar Heel recruit, Perkins replied "Yeah." And that's all. Doherty thought: "I've got to spend four years with this guy?" Perkins, Silent Sam, "Kareem" on the mean-street playgrounds, who was raised as a Jehovah's Witness in Bedford Stuyvesant, struck a friendship with Worthy, who was known by the family name "Ager" and was the son of a Baptist minister and great-grandson of a full-blood Indian, when both played on an international team in Brazil. Jordan, "Rabbit" to his prep buddies, passed up a similar trip to Germany because he wanted to graduate high school with honors. Early on, he was a serious NC *State* fan.

And how heterogeneous their futures! Black, who played in a record 105 Carolina victories, would become a coach; Doherty, the do-everything, nuts and bolts bluecollar yeoman, landed on Wall Street. Even as they lit up professional basketball, Perkins set his sights on TV analysis, Worthy vowed to be an entrepreneur in the cemetery business, and Jordan? Goodness only knows... for what becomes a legend more than he can stick his tongue out at the world and the world love every silver second of him?

For all the rest of Carolina, if the world has been ever full of Spring, 1982, it has been reminded of this team. The feeling being mutual, of course. As an earlier Tar Heel Mitch Kupchak, once said: "When you sign a contract at Carolina, you sign a contract for life."

And on that hazy Louisiana evening when the infant Jordan—is it possible he was only a freshman?— hit the winning basket and the indomitable Worthy stole off like a phantom from Mardi Gras with the winning interception...the same night Henry Fonda finally won his Oscar...and, no less Hollywoodian, Dean Smith finally won his NCAA...on that night all the hard work, deep bruises, late hours struggling back to "The Hall" at Granville South, even the junk snacks at Ken's Quickee Mart...every stressful part that made up the wondrous whole of being a basketball player at Carolina turned out to be worth it.

It was a bond between these young men. Each one sacrificing his individual interests to the team goal, which is what the sport is all about at UNC. Achieving that point of excellence whereby they no longer played merely an opponent but against the game itself. "The year before (losing in the finals to Indiana) it was like we had our knives and forks ready, the napkins in our laps. But nobody brought dinner," said Doherty.

And then: New Orleans, the feast. Where, faithful to his tenets to the end, the coach said to pay attention not to him but to the team: "These are the kinds of players and people who make the job worthwhile," Dean Smith said. "These are the ones you *search* for."

Hugh Morton

Photographer Hugh Morton captured the emptiness and exhaustion that followed the 1982 NCAA championship game against Georgetown. Shown just seconds before they returned to the court for their trophy are (right to left) team captain Jimmy Black, MVP James Worthy (note net around neck), Sports Information Director Rick Brewer, and Head Coach Dean E. Smith.

N.CAROLINA 61
GEORGETOWN 62
poydras street
LANE AND
NORT
23
CAROL
50
GEORGETOWN
32

The shot heard 'round the world: Jordan's jumper beats Georgetown, 63-62.

Allen Steele

Marlboro
N.CAROLINA 63
GEORGETOWN 62
N.CAROLINA
GEORGETOWN

"62-61…Carolina had a 61-60 lead with 1:19 to play…Matt Doherty missed the front end of a one-and-one and Sleepy Floyd scored to put Georgetown ahead…30 seconds left to go…to Jimmy Black on the right side…to Michael Jordan back on the right… over to Jimmy Black…Black, holding high, goes to Doherty… Doherty in the double-team…gives it back to Black with 20 seconds left to play…goes back to Michael Jordan…jumper from out on the left…GOOD!!!…63-62!!!…13, 12, 11… Georgetown with one time-out… Fred Brown…looking…THROW AWAY TO WORTHY!…WORTHY, FIVE…THE TARHEELS ARE GOING TO WIN THE NATIONAL CHAMPIONSHIP!!!…The pass was intercepted by James Worthy!!!…Worthy took the ball away!!!…He had done everything offensively!!!…Oh, wait a minute, Worthy's been fouled…It's an intentional foul…He'll get two shots, I believe… There are two seconds remaining."

Woody Durham, taken from live play-by-play, Louisiana Superdome, March 29, 1982

The clock and the Tar Heel faces are frozen forever in this magical photograph from THE game.

143

Joe Rodriguez

ONE GREAT TEACHER

by Jim Jenkins

I was a member of the In-Between Generation at Chapel Hill, those who matriculated with the dawn of the 1970's. We had been preceded by the "hippies" and were followed by the "yuppies," and we caught the Great University in a transition period of its own, wrestling with its curriculum and purpose. Like the members of our class, the old school seemed a bit confused as to what to do with itself.

The watchword of the day was "relevance," and to achieve it, the faculty and administration adjusted the curriculum to allow students more freedom in choosing their courses of study. Some years later, they would realize this to be a mistake, and return to the traditional smorgasbord of required courses that leave graduates perhaps less relevant, but certainly more educated.

For me, the "relevance" resulted in a series of courses taught by those who, advance intelligence had it, were rather liberal with the academic scoresheet. My early instructors ranged from guys with waist-length beards who mumbled things about the greatness of Eugene McCarthy to young women who felt English was best taught outdoors and accompanied by a guitar. I do not blame the University for this, as many of the roads I traveled were of my choosing.

Fortunately, I happened to stumble down one path not of my choosing which, some 17 years after I entered the University, convinces me that an old sage of the campus was right when he told me: "If you get one great teacher, it will all be worthwhile."

Peter Franklin Walker has no reason to remember me, as the best I could do in his history courses was a Gentleman's C. But when I look on my library shelves, the books I saved from the temptation of selling for date money are those from his courses. When I tell the stories every grad tells of his academic career, the stories I tell are his. When I conjure in my mind the image and the soul of what a teacher is, I see his white shock of hair and hear the strains of his soft, baritone voice and see him still, leaning against his podium, bedecked in his old Army uniform, which I recall he wore on the day he taught a segment on the Civil War battle of Chancellorsville:

"Ladies and gentlemen, I thought it only appropriate that today, as we shall discuss one great battle, I should wear the uniform of a battle long ago, when I was dark of hair and, as you can see, thinner of belly."

There are Baptist preachers who, I have heard it said, can preach hell so hot that you can feel the embers at your feet. Peter Walker taught Chancellorsville in such a manner that you could smell the gunpowder and see the carnage. He taught of characters in history so vividly that they seemed to linger over his shoulder, slightly embarrassed that one man would know so much about them. And he did this not with stage props or disguises or gimmicks, as some professors have been known to do, but with the majesty of his knowledge and the dramatic certainty of his delivery. I know he was a brilliant researcher; I know also he was a deft writer; I could have imagined him as well as an actor. But I shall be forever grateful that he became a teacher. One great teacher.

English Professor J. Lee Greene.

THE PRICE WE ALL MUST PAY FOR QUALITY EDUCATION

by James B. Hunt, Jr.

All North Carolinians are proud of the University of North Carolina at Chapel Hill. In its first 200 years it has become the equivalent of Ivy League universities, with several of its schools being the best, or among the best, in the nation.

And this happened in a largely rural Southern state that did not historically have great families of wealth and centers of capital. It came despite the fact that we have not been the focus of great defense industries, such as happened on the West Coast, Texas, and the Northeast.

This excellence, these stimulating teachers and creative researchers, did not just "happen." We, the people of North Carolina, determined to have them and were willing to pay for them. And what a bargain we got!

That payment was made with our tax money. It amounts to only a few dollars per year for us as individuals, but when our dollars were added together, we had the support for first-rate buildings, equipment and professors. And while North Carolina ranks in the top ten states in per capita financial support for public higher education, I don't believe I have ever heard anyone complain that we are paying too much.

In fact, we have been investing in higher education in North Carolina as a means toward social progress and as a strategic way to pull ourselves up by our bootstraps economically. The Research Triangle would not be here without it. Our microelectronics and medical industries depend on it. It has been a way for North Carolina to get ahead of other states that had more wealth in private hands but who did not focus their resources on brainpower and equal opportunity for their people.

If we are truly thankful for the establishment of Carolina, "America's first public university in 1789," for the past leadership of Frank Porter Graham and Bill Friday, for the great teaching and creation of new knowledge for the progress of mankind at Chapel Hill, then we must *each* show our appreciation. We must volunteer to pay our personal share for this quality education, and we must demand that North Carolina as a state keep its universities among the nation's best.

Our children and our grandchildren must have the opportunity that we had in our generation—to attend Carolina as students and to find there the excitement of learning and the same motivation to make a better state and nation that has made the University of North Carolina at Chapel Hill admired throughout the world.

GEORGE MOSES HORTON

by Robyn Hadley

Just where do I fit into all this? That is a question I asked myself time and again during my childhood years in Graham—years highlighted, I remember, by ravenous reading competitions at the public library. Those formative years of searching, questioning and study prepared me for what would be many happy years in a haven designed especially for inquisitive bookworms like me, that is, the North Carolina Collection in Wilson Library at UNC.

The North Carolina Collection became "my own space," my own special treasure chest containing row after row of books, films, records and maps that opened my eyes to North Carolina, to the world, and to my own identity as a Black woman, a Southerner, a human being and a dreamer. I found many treasures in my hours there, but I especially prize one particular story I found in those stacks—the story of George Moses Horton, the Black bard.

Despite the fact that he was born a slave in the 1790's, George Moses Horton was probably the first Black man of letters in the United States. At a very early age he moved with his master's family to Chatham County, and as a young man he was often sent by his master to Chapel Hill to sell fruit to the students at the University. Many of them laughed at Horton and "sported" with the country slave, but when they forced him to "make speeches" for their amusement, Horton responded—to their astonishment—with original, impromptu poetry.

Horton's fame spread across campus like wildfire, and many a lovesick lad flocked to him so that he might dictate flowery love letters and poems designed to capture the hearts of unsuspecting Southern belles. For prices ranging from 25 cents to 75 cents, depending on the length, Horton created poems that were purchased by such noted patrons as James K. Polk and Joseph Caldwell—men who would later become Presidents of the United States and the University.

One beautiful part of the Horton story is the fact that this famous Black bard could not write. It is not surprising, then, that the purchasing student would list himself as author of the Horton-spun letter or poem. The more I read of Horton's work, the more puzzled I became, for how was it possible to create such prose without seeing it, and editing it, on paper? His secret, he told admirers and patrons, was that he listened very carefully when the Bible and Wesleyan hymns were read and sung at home and at church.

As was the case with many slaves in the 1820's, Horton sought his master's permission to "buy his freedom," to earn enough for his master through hard work that he might be rewarded with passage on a ship bound for Liberia. There, the slave had heard, he could be free of his bonds. While Horton enjoyed his contact with University students and faculty, the daily sixteen-mile walk was onerous, especially on days when he could only find work as a janitor's apprentice. After all, sales for dictated poetry didn't come easy, especially for a poet whose customers were living on students' incomes. "Freedom" would change all that, so Horton set freedom as his goal.

In 1829 Gales and Son of Raleigh printed "Hope of Liberty," a pamphlet of Horton's poems which was sold to raise funds for purchasing his freedom. His master, however, knew a good thing when he saw it, and he raised the required price so high that, despite the effort and support of the University community, the drive fell short of its goal.

"He was a slave who owned his master," Dr. Collier Cobb told a Harvard University audience in 1886, three years after the death of the poet. "Ignorant of the rules of prosody, Horton was a man of letters before he learned to read; a writer of short stories who was published simultaneously in several newspapers before the days of syndication; an author who supported himself and his family in an intellectual center before authorship had attained to the dignity of a profession in America." Some said Horton looked like Othello and "possessed the gravity of a Grecian philosopher." Horton's friend Caroline Hentz, a novelist and wife of a University professor, said that while Horton familiarized himself "with the best of classic works belonging to the fine libraries of the University…he was obliged to be indebted to others for embodying the dream of his Muse."

George Moses Horton, a slave writing about slavery in a slave state. Perhaps the only freedom he ever earned was that he taught himself to write, and eventually he published three books of poetry which bore his name as author. Though he lacked a press agent and, therefore, died virtually unknown outside of Chatham and Orange, Horton's story was somehow preserved for a hundred years in an obscure row of books in "my space," the North Carolina Collection library. I, for one, will be forever indebted to the men and women who saved that story, for George Moses Horton, the Black bard, taught me about the power of human possibility, the strength of ordinary folk. George Moses Horton helped me better understand my world.

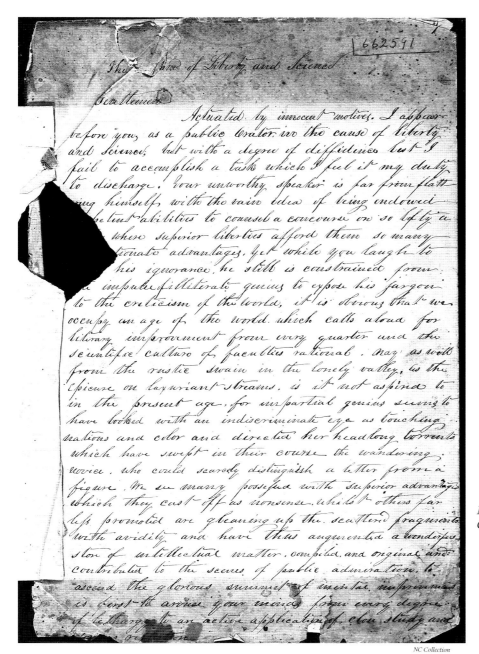

Manuscript penned by the immortal George Moses Horton.

"While tracing thy visage, I sink in emotion,
for no other damsel so wond'rous I see;
Thy looks are so pleasing, thy charms so amazing,
I think of no other, my true-love, but thee."

George Moses Horton
from *The University Magazine*

Dan Charlson

Protest shanties near South Building

THE UNIVERSITY IN 1987: ITS FREEDOMS AND ITS ACHIEVEMENTS

by Christopher C. Fordham, III

I was awakened by a telephone ring shortly after 6:00 A.M. on a Monday in mid-March, 1986. The caller gave his name and indicated that he and a group of other students wished to build makeshift shanties on the Polk Place lawn near the South Building. When I met with the group in my office later that morning, they convinced me that they were sincerely resolved to peaceably educate their fellow students and others about the unconscionable political leadership and the dreadful living conditions in South Africa. Further, they wished to protest the fact that the University owned shares of stock in several companies doing business in South Africa, and they wanted to send a message to the Trustees that those investment holdings should be sold.

As we talked we found ourselves spending a considerable amount of time discussing "freedom," a word which many of us have difficulty defining but a concept for which our founding fathers and millions more have willingly given their lives. As we sat there calmly, rationally discussing all of the dimensions of "freedom," we agreed that freedom is best served when its tension is well-managed, for only then can we have mature freedom.

We talked about other philosophic, human-value, and operational aspects of the protest and its methods. We talked about respecting those with whom we disagree and the importance of permitting the views of all to be heard and respected. This group of students impressed me as serious, thoughtful, trustworthy and thoroughly decent.

After consulting with colleagues, I prepared a response granting the permission for the specific purpose of permitting and facilitating the freedom of expression of this deeply-held view, consistent with the tradition of the institution. The response also stipulated the location of the structures and conditions of maintenance.

Soon thereafter a different student group came forward to protest the existence of the shanties. They indicated their desire to build a "Berlin Wall" to symbolize oppression behind the Iron Curtain, and they asked to locate it on the lawn adjacent to the shanty town as a counter-demonstration. After permission had been granted, the "Berlin Wall" was erected without serious mishap, the dialogue about "mutual respect" went on, and Polk Place accommodated the public expression of these strongly-held views.

This sequence of events largely concerned a kind of freedom resolutely guarded and preserved by and in the University community, i.e., the freedom of expression and its associated First Amendment freedoms. These traditional freedoms, making up what we call political and religious freedom, are fundamental to our democracy and are central to the University's values.

This brief recollection is what some people might call a case study in the exercise of free expression. There are several categories of freedom and there is endless rhetoric devoted to it. It ostensibly is the cornerstone of the great American experiment in democracy, in the evolution of the concepts of political and religious freedom in the Western civilization, and it is surely the bedrock of values of the great University. The case study approach to understanding the freedoms may be of value because it leads to an examination of specifics, and freedom lives and dies when tension-producing conflicts of values are tested. Such conflicts abound in today's society: they relate to censorship, religious freedom, political freedom and academic freedom. Recent events and conflicts in our society suggest that we do not yet understand many of the nuances of freedom, and that true political and religious freedom are still in the process of evolving in our society. So it is not amiss to recapitulate the kinds of freedom which characterize this great institution.

Academic freedom, of course, comes quickly to mind. Deriving primarily from a fundamental need for the scholar to be free to search for the truth and express himself/herself openly and freely, without fear of reprisal, even academic freedom has been under assault in these times. Some view it as a simple and narrow concept relating only to the Constitutionally-guaranteed First Amendment freedoms. Others view it more broadly as freedom to express one's self in a variety of ways and in relationship to a set of responsibilities pertinent to the academic environment. The faculty of a good institution should, for example, exercise freedom and responsibility in the determination of who shall teach, what shall be taught, how it shall be taught, and who shall be admitted to the course of study. Intrusions upon these responsibilities tend to constrain academic freedom just as surely as penalties for the espousing of unpopular views. The concept of academic freedom is still evolving in this country, and it may be that the quality and character of the environment in the exercise of freedom and responsibility are values close to the heart of the issue.

Beyond the First Amendment freedoms, so important to the nature and spirit of the University, there is the extraordinary personal freedom delegated to the students of today's University. The freedom to make choices, take risks, and find one's own values in one's own way is an extraordinary freedom abundantly available to the students of today. Because of some of the social problems which society faces, there is the tendency in some institutions to assert more control over student life and to compromise the personal freedom and choices of students. The spirit of independent student freedom and responsibility at Chapel Hill is so strong and so important that it seems to me entirely unlikely that such trends will have significant force here. The exercise of student freedom and responsibility is an essential part of the growth and maturation of students, and there is no reason to think that it will not continue to work wonders. Appropriate assistance, counsel and advice along the way which tend to be nondirective and nonintrusive are likely to continue to be welcomed by the students.

There is yet a third major freedom associated with the University, sometimes called economic freedom or the "freedom from . . ." A first class college experience, such as that available in Chapel Hill, is quite likely, from experience, to provide its graduates with freedom from primitive material wants, illiteracy, and even undue narrowness of mind and smallness of spirit. This is not an inconsequential freedom, for it may bring the real opportunity of a joyful and satisfying life.

In addition to these notions of freedom in relationship to UNC in 1987, there are many pragmatic reasons why bright and talented students should seize any possible opportunity to study at the University of North Carolina. Why encourage the brightest and most talented students to beat a path to Chapel Hill?

Because the academic resources are awesome. First, the faculty is acknowledged as the outstanding faculty in the southeastern United States according to recent studies published by the National Academy Press. There are more outstanding academic departments in Chapel Hill than anywhere else, and Carolina is the only institution in the Southeast which ranks in the top 20 nationally.

Because the other academic resources are strong. The University research library is the outstanding facility of its type in the Southeast and the only one in our region which ranks in the top 20 nationally. The University library is a magnificent facility with outstanding services.

Because the undergraduate curriculum at the University is up-to-date and outstanding. Authorities outside the state cite the revised undergraduate curriculum at the University of North Carolina as a truly noteworthy advance. The faculty considered, determined and expressed their views and their guidance as to what should constitute a sound and appropriate undergraduate experience in the latter part of the 20th Century. There are few equals.

Because the traditions of student freedom and responsibility encourage the optimum in human growth and development among its students. An array of student organizations and activities provide many opportunities for substantial personal development, growth and maturation.

Because there is an uncommonly good and lively spirit about the place, infectious and enriching. The traditional Carolina spirit is far more than that exemplified near the field of play. It is a noble expression of institutional spirit, one that endures in the lives of its alumni and one that enhances the joy of their lives. The networking which results from these relationships and emanates from this fountainhead of good and lively spirit has, therefore, both pragmatic and philosophic implications.

Because there is beauty to be learned, appreciated and enjoyed. Natural beauty, the beauty of the arts, and the beauty of seeking insight and enlightenment enhance the human spirit.

Because the professional schools and graduate programs of the University are outstanding. In most fields of academic study, a student can go as far as the discipline goes in a program of the highest quality. The undergirding of research programs is extensive and remarkably impressive, with externally-sponsored funding exceeding $100 million per year. The range of research is extremely broad, and the University boasts outstanding graduate and research programs in a wide variety of disciplines, and more than 36 interdisciplinary centers and institutes.

Because extensive outreach programs connect the faculty with the people of the state of North Carolina. The Institute of Government, the Area Health Education Centers Program, the Small Business Development and Technology Center, the Kenan Institute of Private Enterprise, the North Carolina Botanical Gardens, and many other programs bring the faculty of the University into direct personal contact with people, institutions and programs throughout the state, enriching both parties, and making it possible for the faculty to bring their special talents and knowledge fully into the arena of public service. Few research universities in the nation exceed our own in the extensiveness, quality and usefulness of these programs.

These dimensions comprise the 20th Century state-owned research University. Perhaps not all things to all people, but . . . almost. The University, as an institution, uniquely apposes the democratic ideals of our society with the achievement of excellence. This high purpose is achieved in the best traditions of the people of North Carolina and as a challenge and model to its youth. Surely it is among the finest institutions which modern mankind has produced, and surely we North Carolinians will continue to support, advance and strengthen its excellence and its contributions to the state and nation.

A scrap of bland, nondescript carpet is transformed into a one-of-a-kind creation of color and symmetry through the masterful brush strokes of Barbara Coon, a graduate student in the Master of Fine Arts program.

Acting requires strict concentration, and the skill of juggling helps to develop it. One practitioner is Thom Garvey, a first-year student in the Master of Fine Arts program, which is tied to the PlayMakers Repertory.

THE FUTURE OF THE UNIVERSITY

by William C. Friday, as told to Tom Wicker

Wicker: President Friday, would you tell me where you think the University is going, or what it should become?

Friday: Well, I start with several basic notions. One is that everybody shouldn't go to college. That's a misapprehension that's gotten abroad because of the advocacy of public universities. A lot of people aren't capable of benefiting from higher education, or don't want it. And in some of the larger institutions there's a drop-out rate in entering classes of 50 percent. Ohio State, for example. So everybody shouldn't go to college.

Second, in this state we have 16 degree-granting publicly-funded universities. That means there is room for a distribution of people and functions. In the last 14 years, we've restricted doctoral training, for example, to Chapel Hill, N.C. State, Greensboro and, to the extent that medical education is involved, East Carolina. That's an important point because doctoral level training is by far the most expensive thing we do.

We have duplicated openly and gladly at the undergraduate level in arts and sciences and across the whole spectrum because we believe very deeply that these young people, these undergraduates, should know something about the world they're in, have some knowledge of history, know something about the English language and be able to use it well. We've worked hard to develop these programs to a level of high quality.

The result is a system of allocated functions, including significant non-academic but essentially related functions—like the operation of a hospital at Chapel Hill, the operation of the Agricultural Extension Service at Raleigh, and so on. It works because there is harmony among our campuses today, and the campuses have benefited because they've gained more resources from the legislature. It works better to go over there as a family of institutions and stand back to back on one very comprehensive program that takes the entire state as its province.

As Edward Kidder Graham said years ago, "The boundaries of this institution are coterminous to the borders of the state." We've never forgotten that and I think that's the University's strength—the state's people relate to it. They come here for medical attention, or they come here as poor kids and get a chance to go to college. And we go to them with public television and with clinics and short courses and specialized training and highway safety and water resources and marine sciences.

We've toted up that we actually touched in one program or another almost a million citizens of this state last year. That's direct, personal involvement. That's not characteristic of most public universities.

But the important thing for the University is to remain true to its purpose. In this state, more today than ever before, the University has to be the center of intellectual ferment, a place where cherished things are contained and made better. The place has to be kept green. To steal John Gardner's line, it has to play the role of loving critic. And if it defaults in that, the state suffers, not just the University. And that doesn't mean irresponsible, undisciplined work, it means a courageous analytical approach to problem-solving and to a society and a people that are still developing. That's what Howard Odum did and that's what Albert Coates did, what Paul Green did in *his* way. That's the tradition of this place.

It would lose its character as a unique institution if it ever lost that. If you can't believe in these things, wait until they're taken away. And this is where the alumni are so important, because there's something you and I can do as citizens. We can all talk to the lawmakers and say, "Now don't do that."

I will never forget working with a well-known writer here in Chapel Hill. This man was never known for discretion. Once at a party, there was a legislator there, and he'd had a drink—I don't know what came up but the writer turned to the legislator and said, "I just want to tell you one thing: you keep your dirty hands off this place." I heard him. He looked at me and he winked and I walked away. I knew there was going to be an argument.

The University serves the individual, that's the important thing. Edward Kidder Graham started it. And Frank Graham, and the rest of us who have come behind them have been able to put a brick in here and there.

Wicker: Are you expecting large growth of the student body?

Friday: Well, at the end of 10 years I would think the enrollment probably will have gone up about 5 percent. But unless there's a dramatic change in attitude we won't exceed that. That's all campuses, all purposes. And that will be at all age levels. We don't think now of entering students as aged 18 to 20; we have students enroll when they're 45, who come for night courses, for health sciences, law, everything.

What we're planning for in these next few years is to concentrate on qualitative growth. We moved so fast during the years after World War II to absorb the veterans, to absorb the growth that this state had experienced, to accommodate growth caused by the Research Triangle, these kinds of things, that it was just absolutely necessary to respond. Now the University has a little breathing room, and the emphasis is going to be on upgrading all the way around.

Wicker: I take it, therefore, that you see this University remaining primarily an educational and service institution for the state and not a big research institution. I don't mean that it will slight research, but that's not going to become its primary function?

Friday: The balance we have among teaching, research and public service will remain about what it is, but all will become better. The public service aspect obviously will have to reflect technological developments, population shifts, scientific advancements—all these things enter into what you do. But we must be out there helping people to find a better way of life, helping them enjoy life, find jobs, create jobs. I think that's an important function and I make no apology for that. I think it's one of the reasons that people in this state speak of this University so well. They can be conservative at home, but they want the University doing what it's doing and they're proud of it.

Wicker: If I take you correctly, you want the University to remain fundamentally centered on teaching.

Friday: Teaching, research, and service as it can be derived from those two.

Wicker: Do you put teaching deliberately first?

Friday: Yes, but teaching and research are not mutually exclusive. We want the good research man to be in the classroom.

Wicker: What's the basic tuition here now at Chapel Hill?

Friday: $772 tuition and fees, if you're an in-state student. If you're an out-of-state student, it's more, one of the highest in the country for a public university. It's $2,600, something like that.

Our policy for the freshman class is 85 percent in-state enrollment. We stick to that because it's very important, we think. That's one place the General Assembly pays attention, among other things. They're very sensitive on that. There is no restriction for out-of-state students at the upper levels or in graduate schools, so it washes out to a rational balance between in and out-of-state, to give the young people a chance at cross-contacts.

And there's another reason. We have a lot of North Carolinians who go to other states. We don't offer everything, and we shouldn't. So it's a matter of reciprocity where we all benefit.

The University has reasserted its relationship with the public schools and Chancellor Fordham deserves a lot of credit for it. We are involved with math and science teachers. We're bringing the principals of the schools here in classes of 45 to learn about their jobs and become more effective.

Wicker: I have focused you on the future. But as you look back now, as you're getting ready to retire, what would you say was the most fundamental challenge you faced, to what you have described as the tradition and function of the University? Was it financial? Was it political?

Friday: It's more than one thing. You have to keep your eye on certain fundamental points. First, keep the University free, keep it open, keep it financed as basically as you can and keep it a vital, dynamic place with a sense of creative involvement. If you can do those things, all the other things will follow. If you have to choose a word, say it's got to be alive.

The big challenge the University has is in keeping its fundamental qualities where they are, assuming a little greater national involvement. It's got to do that. And, before this century's over, the University will be international in ways that it doesn't conceive of right now. I wouldn't venture to know how many countries we're involved with—contractual relationships, student exchanges. When you and I came to college—well, I don't know about you—but I didn't know there was very much of a world the other side of the Catawba River. But each of my children had been to Europe at least once, if not twice, before they ever set foot in college.

So you have a much more sophisticated student, maybe with a juvenile point of view to begin with. But my kids can talk to me about what they saw in Paris and Rome and Venice in a way I used to talk about Kings Mountain and Stanley Creek. I didn't have that opportunity and I am thankful that I could provide it for them. And that's what most people forget when they talk about this generation. They're just not on the same wave-length as these kids.

People say, "But what's wrong with this generation? It doesn't say anything." This generation knows more and they're looking at us with questions: "Why haven't you been there? What's your basis of understanding and judgment?" And that, I think, is an enormous asset that this generation of Americans has. It's going to be very beneficial in time, and we ought to provide, through the universities of this country, a chance for it to grow and develop.

Wicker: I'd like to ask you about the time of the Speaker Ban and your fight against that. Do you think the state learned something from that, that now that kind of pressure on academic freedom—on freedom, not just academic freedom—is diminished, not just because some years have passed but because something was learned?

Friday: Something was learned by *that* generation. But what you're witnessing right now in this Accuracy in Academia movement is a revival in a new generation of the notion that education is not to be trusted. The clash of ideas, the open and uninhibited confrontation, is a fundamental element of a university's existence, and the only alternative is to admit that you're afraid to discuss an idea. If you admit that, then you're going in the other direction about as fast as you can go.

I don't believe most thoughtful Americans will ever admit that this country is so weak it can't discuss ideas. We've got to say it out loud, though, that we're strong enough. It isn't being said enough.

Wicker: I understand that about 40 percent of the students on the Chapel Hill campus get some kind of financial assistance?

Friday: About that. Interestingly enough, we still have large numbers of young people who are the first college students in their families. It shows you how far we have to go. This state, with all that it does at the upper levels, is not even at the national average of college-age attendance. We have only 40 percent. Now that's an economic statistic this state can't afford. That's as solid a reason for investment of tax dollars in a university as I know of, because it's self-serving, you get your talent back. It's income-producing, it's taxpaying, and it's law abiding in most cases. That's what they're looking for.

Wicker: Will the historically black college continue to exist?

Friday: It must. Because what we've done with the civil rights movement is create a level of expectation that is, I think, very important to satisfy. In the last 15 years, this University System has tried to be accountable to the moral obligation to provide, at least at the undergraduate level, parity of institutions at the minimum base. That is, the same salary scale, library, buildings, all this. And we've achieved this.

The problem is one that reaches back to the family, in terms of preparation.

What does a student bring to the process in terms of personal knowledge, development? Here's where you see the marked differences in individuals. But that is not an argument to deny opportunity. And that's why I would say that for the next generation, we're going to keep good, solid black schools, with substantial mixing of whites. Fifteen percent minimum is what by law the mix must be. Whether it'll be more or not depends on whether it's in a metropolitan region. The Fayetteville campus has more than 15 percent.

In the long perception, how do you want to see a society right itself? In my view, you start with the education of your people. There is no substitute, I'm convinced of that. I've watched it too long.

You can't be held accountable for the fact that you were born where you were. It's not your fault you're poor. That's what rankles me most, the assumption of government that I am what I am because of who I am, and I didn't try. I never had a chance to try. I can get indignant about this because I was born and grew up in the Depression and I lived in Gaston County. I saw those squads go from building to building, mill to mill and close them down, and people get in bread lines . . . well, the fact that I can tell you that so vividly today tells you what an impression it made on me.

This is an important part of the report of the North Carolina 2000 Commission, the one they asked me to chair. We listed the five things people felt most keenly about. By a 3 to 1 vote, out of 125,000 people we canvassed, it was education. Even if it meant greater taxes.

Wicker: What were the other four?

Friday: Economic opportunity, jobs; the environment and its maintenance, fresh air, clean water. The fourth one was natural resource preservation because that's the basis of the tourist industry and all that spins from that. Fifth was personal security, police protection.

The public has some ideas about its own future that it didn't think about 25 years ago. And that, I think, is the healthiest thing of all. If we can believe that there is thinking going on and that we're having some impact to stimulate it, then this University is fulfilling one of its major requirements, to keep people aware that they do have an impact, that they do have a voice—and don't run from it, don't shirk that obligation. Get up and speak your mind!

I feel all this very strongly because I know that my chance to influence is not going to be here next year in this position. I have to find another vehicle to work from. But I intend to keep on. I really feel, for the first time in my life, I really feel that it's come together for me. I see how these things integrate and I get around enough and I've been at it long enough so that people will pull me in to be a part of something where ordinarily they wouldn't let someone in. In that sense, it's really a very exciting role to play—I get really involved with these people and I think there's an enormous asset there that the state ought to husband as carefully as it can.

Steve Muir

Steve Auer

A student in Studio Art, Marc Leuthold examines a portion of his imaginative ceramic sculpture for which he has joined a progression of gear-like shapes fashioned from lifeless slabs of clay.

The Old Well hasn't moved in years, but graduate student Greg Turk can rotate it by using the Computer Science department's Pixel-planes machine. It is one of the results of the microelectronic initiative in North Carolina, for it rapidly generates realistic images of three-dimensional scenes — shadows and all.

A big horn provides a big sound and David Barman practices his tuba to bring to the orchestra his complementary notes.

Lorraine Leigh, co-captain of the Women's Fencing Team for 1987-88, assumes a position of "on guard" with a "point-in-line." The women's and men's teams, coached by Ron Miller, finished the season with respective records of 18-5 and 18-7.

Steve Muir

Steve Muir

THE AUTHORS

Smith Barrier, class of 1937, has authored more than 10,000 sports stories in his distinguished career. A resident of Greensboro, Barrier is a semi-sort-of-retired freelancer who (according to Furman Bisher) "spent at least 70 or 80 years on the staff of the *News and Record.*"

Kemp Plummer Battle, class of 1849, served as President of the University during the trying years of reconstruction/reopening that followed the Civil War. History tells us that he was insightful, witty, and abundantly tolerant and fair. Battle was also the University's most prolific historian.

Denton native *Furman Bisher,* UNC '38, has long been Atlanta's leading sports authority. According to Smith Barrier, this globe-trotting *Journal* sports editor "has covered every major sporting event from the World Series to the Olympic Games at least 100 times apiece."

Eric R. Calhoun, class of 1969, married the Chancellor's daughter (the lovely Mary Sitterson) and "took off for the good life of the Wyoming mountains." Fifteen years later we found him behind a vice president's desk at Richardson Corporation in Greensboro — grayer, with *much* shorter hair, and the proud papa of four.

Branded for life with the nickname "Scoop," *Orville B. Campbell,* class of 1942, has been a quiet, guiding force behind nearly every worthwhile statewide project of the past 40 years. Publisher of the *Chapel Hill Newspaper,* Campbell is a celebrated composer, printer, fundraiser, record album producer, golfer, and former *Tar Heel* editor.

A.J. Carr, an award-winning sportswriter with the *Raleigh News and Observer,* hails from Wallace, which is almost as big as A.J.'s newspaper building. The affable Mr. Carr guesstimates that he's written more than 1,000 columns on the men in blue during his 21 years at the *N&O.*

One of the most respected members of the North Carolina General Assembly, *Marie Colton* of Asheville is a member of the class of 1943. She is described by friends as "a wonderful mother and wife, a leader with an inexhaustible supply of energy, and a mover and shaker when something important needs doing."

Soft-spoken gentleman of gentlemen, *Dr. Archie K. Davis* of Winston-Salem, class of 1932, has excelled in at least four fields that we know of, and there are probably others: Chairman of the Board of Wachovia Bank and Trust Company, State Senator, founding father of the Research Triangle Park, and noted American historian.

Douglas S. Dibbert, UNC '70, serves as Executive Director of the Carolina General Alumni Association. While at the University Dibbert was elected to Phi Beta Kappa, Phi Eta Sigma, the Order of the Golden Fleece, and the Order of the Old Well.

Woody Durham, class of 1963, is the never-say-die "Voice of the Tar Heels." Despite the fact that his play-by-play announcing is ever so slightly biased in favor of the team in light blue, Woody has enjoyed great success in broadcasting. In a period of just ten years he rose from reporter to news director to network executive.

During his lifetime *Sam J. Ervin, Jr.,* UNC '17, was North Carolina's best-loved and most internationally prominent public servant. As a judge and later as Chairman of the Senate Watergate Committee, Ervin insisted on truth, freedom, and — as often as possible — wholesome, knee-slapping humor.

As a senior *Phil Ford, Jr.,* UNC 1978, was an Olympic gold medalist and NCAA Player of the Year. A deadly shooter and incomparable point guard, this favorite son of Rocky Mount starred for NBA teams in Kansas City, Milwaukee and Houston.

Greensboro native *Christopher C. Fordham, III,* class of 1947, enjoyed a brilliant career in medicine before becoming Chancellor of the University. Students particularly admire the fact that Chancellor Fordham seeks out meetings with them — sessions in which they say he listens intently to their concerns, always respecting the fact that they, too, are adults.

Hailed by many as the most admired man in North Carolina, *William Clyde Friday,* 1948 LLB, has been presented every prestigious award imaginable within the field of higher education. During his 30-year tenure as President of the University, Bill Friday served as an educational advisor to numerous U.S. Presidents. He and his charming wife Ida were voted North Carolina Public Servants of the Year in 1980.

Kays Gary, UNC '42, certainly ranks as one of the most popular newspaper columnists in the state, and he even has a large following of readers in South Carolina. Ever clever and perceptive, Gary has won many awards for his *Charlotte Observer* columns because they prompt readers to see themselves as they really are—and to laugh in spite of it.

One of the great tributes to *Dr. Frank Porter Graham,* class of 1909, is this: When polled, many of the University's present-day leaders agreed that "Dr. Frank" is the school's most distinguished and influential alumnus.

Mount Airy native *Andy Griffith,* class of 1949, will likely be just as popular with television audiences in 2087 as he is in 1987. The King of the "fifedom" known as Rerun (which is a suburb of Mayberry), Sheriff Andy is *the* best-known graduate in UNC history for, after all, he's said, "Sarah, this is Andy. . . .Get me the diner, please. . . ." in English, French, Spanish, German, Japanese, Swedish. . . .

The pride of Alamance County, *Robyn Hadley* of Graham, class of 1985, is a Rhodes Scholar currently holed up in a library somewhere in Oxford, England. If she sets her mind to it, she will someday be the state's first female Governor or U.S. Senator.

Grace Hamrick of Shelby, UNC '41, is a talented journalist and super-charged community volunteer. Grace is also the only woman to have held the post of President of the UNC General Alumni Association.

Raleigh's *Chip Henderson* is one of North Carolina's most recognized commercial photographers. He and Steve Muir head Henderson/Muir Photography and recently opened their new 7,000 square-foot studio. Noted designer *Russell Avery* and associate editor *Jane Collins* have collaborated with the photographers to produce several award-winning picture books: most recently was *Early Comes The Sun,* a pictorial book featuring coastal North Carolina.

North Carolina's only two-term Governor, *James B. Hunt, Jr.* of Rock Ridge graduated from UNC's Law School in 1964. Eminently qualified to speak on the subject of higher education, Jim is the Chairman of the prestigious National Board for Professional Teaching Standards.

An expert on everything that's funny about the Tar Heel State, *Jim Jenkins* of Raleigh, class of 1974, was the *Greensboro News and Record's* wittiest columnist before he moved to the *Raleigh News and Observer* to try his hand at editorial writing.

Charlie Justice, UNC '50, is a Cherryville insurance executive who was everything a football coach ever dreamed of, and more. In the post-World War II years "Choo Choo" was the most popular and publicized college athlete in America.

Although *John F. Kennedy* did not attend UNC, his spirit and presence are still felt on campus to this day. Had he been asked to write a Foreword for this book, President Kennedy might have said, "This is a history of men and women who asked, 'What can I do for Carolina and my country?' rather than 'What can Carolina and America do for me?'"

Dr. Arnold K. King, UNC '25, devoted his professional career to the improvement of higher education, and the University community will be forever indebted to him for his tireless dedication as a Vice President, professor, and school historian.

Curry Kirkpatrick, class of 1965, is a Senior Editor for *Sports Illustrated* magazine. His jealous classmates marvel at the fact that he is able to cover the world of college basketball from his home on the beach of Hilton Head Island.

The editor of the 1955 *Tar Heel, Charles B. Kuralt* is viewed by many as America's finest broadcast journalist. The recipient of nearly every major television award available, Charles successfully blazed new television trails with his popular "On the Road" and "Sunday Morning" programs.

Margaret Palmer Lauterer, class of 1967, left her native Crossnore for the bright lights of Chapel Hill and, in short order, a successful career in photojournalism. "Maggie," who says she'll someday write a novel about Eleanor Swain and the Yankee brigadier, hangs her hat (and camera and typewriter) at the *Citizen-Times* in Asheville.

A past Alumni Association President, *Hugh Morton,* 1943, of Linville has won national and international awards for his creative filmmaking and photography. The former photo editor of both the *Yack* and the *Tar Heel,* Morton and his wife Julia (in her 13th year on the UNC Board of Governors) have known the joy of having all four of their children enrolled at the great University.

Hugh Morton, Jr., class of 1970, is the little tyke shown with Chancellor House on page 72 herein. Morton edited this book and two others in the seventies and eighties before taking the position of State Travel and Tourism Director in Raleigh.

Winston-Salem's *Karen Parker,* class of 1965, is now an editor with the *Los Angeles Times.* Many of her classmates have threatened to form a committee to bring Karen, Andy Griffith, Charles Scott, Mitch Kupchak and James Worthy back from California to Chapel Hill (where they belong, by gosh!).

Neale Patrick, UNC '39, holds some sort of record for attendance at Carolina football games. Beginning with his years as a student, the popular sports editor of the *Gastonia Gazette* attended *every* Tar Heel home game for approximately 42 years! Let's see . . . that converts to 23,683 passes, 17,652 punts, 273 halftime shows . . . .

Durham's *Sibyl Goerch Powe* may just be *the* class of 1947. She is a former newspaper reporter, Secretary of the State Democratic Party, General Alumni Association board member, Morehead Scholarship committee member, Board of Visitors member, member of the Order of the Tar Heel 100 . . . and the list goes on and on.

Terry Sanford, UNC '39, has distinguished himself and the University by serving in the Federal Bureau of Investigation, as the Governor of North Carolina, as Duke's President, and in the U.S. Senate. He has done *so* well, in fact, that he is claimed as a native son by Laurinburg, Fayetteville, Raleigh and Durham.

Julian Scheer, class of 1950, is a country gentleman in that horsey area of northern Virginia. A Senior Vice President of LTV Corporation, Scheer is a former award-winning columnist, author, and NASA executive whose influence was etched for the ages when a North Carolina mountain peak was named in his honor in the fifties.

The pride of the class of 1970, *Charles T. Scott* is a successful businessman/entrepreneur in Hollywood, California. His remarkable feats in a Carolina uniform overshadowed his accomplishments in the classroom (where he earned *Academic* All-America honors).

Although he is a Kansan, *Dean E. Smith* has more friends than any other man who ever called North Carolina home. By any standard or measure, Coach Smith and his friend John Wooden of UCLA are the most successful basketball coaches in NCAA history.

Irrepressible phrase-turner *A.C. Snow,* UNC '50, has somehow found time to edit the *Raleigh Times* six days a week for the past umpteen years. His friends and classmates wish for him the fulfillment of his lifelong dream: a cozy cottage amid the tall pines of Chapel Hill.

Builder, banker, board member, and brilliant businessman *C.D. "Dick" Spangler,* class of 1954, became the President of the University on October 12, 1986. In keeping the University ship on its same steady course, President Spangler has brought his own special dignity and exciting energy to his new position.

The late *Walter Spearman,* class of 1929, is profiled in this volume as one of the most honored and respected students in the school's history. It is to his and the University's great credit that he later became one of the institution's most admired professors.

Morehead Scholar *Gray Temple, Jr.,* class of 1965, has been an Episcopal clergyman since 1968. He serves as Rector of Saint Patrick's Episcopal Church in Atlanta, and he also works closely with St. Luke's Cathedral in Butere, Kenya. Wonder if he got down on his knees during the last minute of the Georgetown game?

Although nearly every U.S. astronaut has been trained in Chapel Hill, *Dr. William E. Thornton,* class of 1952, is to date the only Carolina graduate to venture into Space. Many of the innovations and techniques developed by Thornton and other doctors at N.C. Memorial Hospital will make interstellar travel more efficient and pleasurable for the next generation of Tar Heels.

What if *Bob Timberlake,* class of 1959, had majored in Art instead of Industrial Relations? In fact, it was not until eleven years after his graduation that Bob became a professional artist. Since making that career change he has learned the art of painting well enough to be honored by Presidents Carter and Reagan in the White House and Prince Charles in Buckingham Palace.

For more than 65 years the late *Hazel Trimble,* class of 1925, was a mainstay of charitable and civic projects in Chapel Hill. Greenthumbed gardener, gifted storyteller, and good neighbor to all, Hazel sort of winked at life and had fun with it for all of her 91 years.

C.J. Underwood, class of 1962, is a Raleigh native who found fame and fortune under the tower of WBTV in Charlotte. His more than 1,000 Kuraltesque profiles of interesting Tar Heel personalities and places have taken him from Lizard Lick to Loafer's Glory. Friends say that he is, and always has been, the best pool player in Mecklenburg County.

Award-winning journalist *Tom Wicker,* class of 1948, is a syndicated columnist with the *New York Times.* The University community is grateful that Tom has often found time to return to Chapel Hill and contribute his spirit and spark to a wide spectrum of seminars, symposiums, and school publications.

The late *Louis Round Wilson,* class of 1899, unselfishly shared half a century of his remarkable life in the service of the University. Librarian, historian, author and scholar, Wilson was admired nationally and internationally by educators, graduates and fellow faculty members.

(The editors express their undying gratitude to these talented men and women for their contributions to this pictorial history of America's first state university. Those authors not pictured above are shown elsewhere in the book. Photographs credited "NC Collection" were generously provided by the North Carolina Collection, UNC Library at Chapel Hill.)

Chip Henderson

The stately, enduring columns of Graham Memorial, completed in 1931 to answer Edward Kidder Graham's desire for a student center, now mark the entrance of the Dramatic Arts building. Though president of the University only a few years, Graham contributed significantly to his alma mater in his short lifetime. His is an example of the leadership and legacy that have brought the University of North Carolina to its place of national and international prominence.